BTEC Level 3 National Study Skills Guide in IT

Welcome to your Study Skills Guide! You can make it your own – start by adding your personal and course details below...

Learner's name: _____

BTEC course title: _____

Date started: _____

Mandatory units:

_____

_____

_____

Optional units:

_____

_____

_____

_____

Centre name: _____

Centre address:

_____

_____

_____

Tutor's name: _____

Published by Pearson Education Limited, a company incorporated in England and Wales, having its registered office at Edinburgh Gate, Harlow, Essex, CM20 2JE. Registered company number: 872828

Edexcel is a registered trademark of Edexcel Limited

Text © Pearson Education Limited 2010

First published 2010

13 12 11

10 9 8 7 6 5 4 3

British Library Cataloguing in Publication Data

A catalogue record for this book is available from the British Library

ISBN 978 1 84690 565 0

Typeset and edited by Ken Vail Graphic Design, Cambridge
Cover design by Visual Philosophy, created by eMC Design
Cover photo/illustration © Shutterstock: Yuri Arcurs
Printed in Great Britain by Ashford Colour Press Ltd

Acknowledgements

The publisher would like to thank the following for their kind permission to reproduce their photographs:

(Key: b-bottom; c-centre; l-left; r-right; t-top)

Alamy Images: Angela Hampton Picture Library 17, Adrian Sherratt 7, Image Source 61, Claudia Wiens 66; **Corbis:** 76, Jutta Klee 10; **iStockphoto:** Chris Schmidt 31; **Pearson Education Ltd:** Steve Shott 26, Ian Wedgewood 59; **Photolibrary.com:** Christa Stadtler 84

Cover images: *Front:* **Shutterstock:** Yuri Arcurs

Every effort has been made to contact copyright holders of material reproduced in this book. Any omissions will be rectified in subsequent printings if notice is given to the publishers.

Websites

Go to www.pearsonhotlinks.co.uk to gain access to the relevant website links and information on how they can aid your studies. When you access the site, search for either the title BTEC Level 3 National in IT or ISBN 9781846905650.

Disclaimer

This material has been published on behalf of Edexcel and offers high-quality support for the delivery of Edexcel qualifications.

This does not mean that the material is essential to achieve any Edexcel qualification, nor does it mean that it is the only suitable material available to support any Edexcel qualification. Edexcel material will not be used verbatim in setting any Edexcel examination or assessment. Any resource lists produced by Edexcel shall include this and other appropriate resources.

Copies of official specifications for all Edexcel qualifications may be found on the Edexcel website: www.edexcel.com

Contents

Popular progression pathways

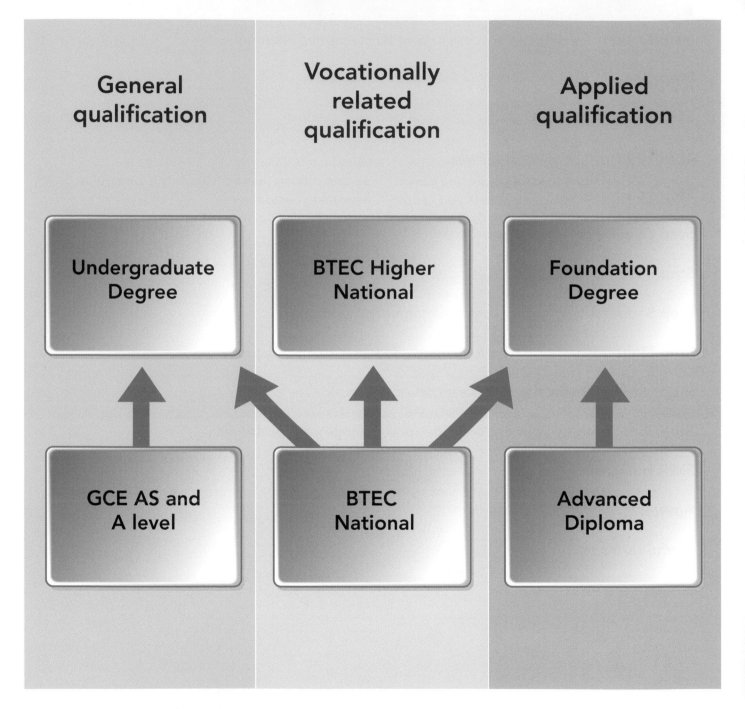

Ten steps to success in your BTEC Level 3 National

This Study Skills Guide has been written to help you achieve the best result possible on your BTEC Level 3 National course. At the start of a new course you may feel both quite excited but also a little apprehensive. Taking a BTEC Level 3 National qualification has many benefits and is a major stepping stone towards your future career. Using this Study Skills Guide will help you get the most out of your course from the start.

TOP TIP

Use this Study Skills Guide at your own pace. Dip in to find what you need. Look back at it whenever you have a problem or query.

During **induction** sessions at the start of your course, your tutor will explain important information, but it can be difficult to remember everything and that's when you'll find this Study Skills Guide invaluable. Look at it whenever you want to check anything related to your course. It provides all the essential facts you need and has a Useful terms section to explain specialist terms, words and phrases, including some that you will see highlighted in this book in bold type.

This Study Skills Guide covers the skills you'll need to do well in your course — such as managing your time, researching and analysing information and preparing a presentation.

- Use the **Top tips** to make your life easier as you go.
- Use the **Key points** to help you to stay focused on the essentials.
- Use the **Action points** to check what you need to know or do now.
- Use the **Case studies** to relate information to your chosen sector and vocational area.
- Use the **Activities** to test your knowledge and skills.
- Use the **Useful terms** section to check the meaning of specialist terms.

This Study Skills Guide has been designed to work alongside the Edexcel Student Book for BTEC Level 3 National IT (Edexcel, 2010). This Student Book includes the main knowledge you'll need, with tips from BTEC experts, Edexcel assignment tips, assessment activities and up-to-date case studies from industry experts, plus handy references to your Study Skills Guide.

This Study Skills Guide is divided into ten steps, each relating to a key aspect of your studies, from understanding assessment to time management to maximising opportunities. Concentrate on getting things right one step at a time. Thousands of learners have achieved BTEC Level 3 National qualifications and are now studying for a degree, or building a successful career at work. Using this Study Skills Guide, and believing in your own abilities, will help you achieve your future goals, too.

Introduction to the IT sector

IT is an exciting and fast-moving area at the forefront of technological development and, unlike some areas of technology, it has a direct impact on our everyday lives. IT is a very wide-ranging area covering everything from games to industrial robots, so there are many different options for specialist topics. IT is used in almost every business and industry you can think of, so you may be able to combine other interests with your interest in IT. For example, if you are interested in music, then you could get involved in the computer programs used to create and edit tracks or to DJ.

Generally, people who work with IT can be divided into users and professionals. Users are people who use IT as a tool to do something. For example, they might watch a video, write a letter or search for something on the internet. Users are not normally technical experts. IT professionals, on the other hand, are the people who make IT work; they are technical experts. The BTEC National is aimed at people who want to become IT professionals, not just users.

As IT is such a wide-ranging sector, at some point you will need to specialise. Your school or college may have already focused your BTEC National course in a particular area by selecting certain optional units. This is sometimes called a 'pathway' and you may be given a choice of different pathways (with different optional units).

The BTEC National has a number of different pathways:

Software development – aimed at learners who are interested in a career designing, writing and testing computer programs.

Networking and systems support – the focus is on computer support, including building, upgrading and repairing systems and networking, including installing, configuring and troubleshooting local and wide area networks.

Business – aimed at learners who are interested in how IT affects businesses, including major issues in business such as e-commerce, security and how future IT developments may affect business.

Open pathway – there is no specific focus; centres can choose the optional units they consider to be most suited to their resources and learners, or may create their own pathway, for example a computer games focus can be created by selecting the optional units which focus on this area.

Software development is a complex and highly technical area and most people who work as programmers have continued their studies to university level. To be a good programmer you need a certain type of mind, able to deal with the complex abstract concepts of programming languages. Many areas of programming, such as games programming, also require a good understanding of mathematics.

Networking and systems support tends to be more practical in its nature and involves carrying out tasks such as installing, configuring and troubleshooting computer and networking hardware. It also relates closely to a number of other areas including IT security and, increasingly, mobile technologies. Trainee and junior positions in this sector can

involve fairly basic tasks (such as manning an IT help desk taking calls from users who have problems with their computer system), but with experience you can begin to move into more engaging and challenging areas.

The business pathway is aimed at learners who want to work alongside a company that is not in the IT sector specifically but which makes extensive use of IT. This might involve helping the firm develop its use of databases to store essential business information, such as customer records or stock levels, developing a web strategy to allow its customers to purchase goods or services online, or developing security systems to protect it from online fraud, viruses and other threats. To work in this area you will need a good understanding of business processes and relevant technology.

In reality these pathways are very broad and can be further subdivided into different areas. For example, software development covers web development, games programming, applications programming, low-level programming (e.g. writing device drivers for new hardware) and many other areas. At this stage in your education you should be considering which area you are most interested in, so that when you come to choose a university course or job you will have a better idea of what you would like to specialise in.

You might follow a software development pathway with units focused on designing and developing software. Alternatively, you could follow a more general approach with a range of units covering different aspects of IT. You can then choose to specialise when you move on to university.

Whichever area of IT interests you the most, you can be sure that there are aspects of it that are exciting and technologically innovative, and that it will give you plenty of scope to develop the skills and knowledge you need in order to enter a fascinating and well-paid career. However, to get the best and most interesting jobs you need to work hard because employers are very demanding. You will need to spend time reading and researching to develop your understanding of this complex technology. Just cruising and getting the pass grades will not get you very far in the IT industry.

Skills for your sector

As you might expect, technical skills are important in the IT sector and, as already mentioned, possessing skills in a particular specialist area is more important than just having a broad range of general skills. However, with IT being such a wide-ranging and fast-changing industry, employers won't necessarily expect you to have detailed technical knowledge in the area for which they are recruiting. Instead, they will look for adaptability and a willingness to learn new skills quickly. In order to judge how good you are at picking up new skills, employers may look at the grades you have achieved in your BTEC National units. For example, if you have gained a Distinction in a unit which might only be vaguely related to the skills they are looking for, they may take that to mean you could quickly gain the new skills required for the job.

Because many jobs for IT professionals involve working alongside IT users – supporting their needs and exchanging information with them – good communication and customer service skills are essential. This means that you must be able to communicate clearly in spoken and written English and have good listening skills. You will also need to be patient and understanding.

Skills IT employers value most
General technical skills

As an IT professional you will be expected to have a solid range of general technical skills and knowledge. This includes knowledge of how to set up and use the most popular operating systems (e.g. the latest Windows operating system), good applications skills for the most commonly used business applications (e.g. Microsoft Office, Internet Explorer, email, etc). You will also be expected to have a good understanding of important IT issues and technologies such as security, wireless networking, the internet, etc. As the IT sector is constantly evolving, you will need to keep up to date with the latest developments and hot topics by reading around the subject.

Specific technical skills

As explained, employers won't always expect you to have deep technical skills in the area of expertise for which they are recruiting, but will look for evidence that you can pick these skills up quickly. If you are interested in getting a job in a particular area, such as web development, you will need to show that you have an interest in that area and have gone beyond the requirements of the relevant units you have studied. For example, you might develop your own website or pick up additional skills while on a work experience placement.

Working in the IT industry requires many technical skills. Your BTEC course will help you to develop some of these skills.

Numeracy and literacy

All employers rate these skills very highly and, in order to help you develop your skills in these areas, you may be studying Functional Skills Maths and English alongside your IT course. It is essential that you should be able to deal with everyday mathematical problems (such as arithmetic, percentages, etc.) and write using proper grammar, punctuation and spelling. In IT you also need to be able to read and understand technical information and be able to write clear technical descriptions.

Customer service skills

Many IT jobs, especially in the area of system support, require employees to possess strong customer-facing skills. End users of IT systems often find these systems difficult and frustrating to use, so you need to be able to assist these users in a sympathetic manner and be able to give them clear, non-technical explanations of how to deal with problems.

IT employers value a range of other attributes. You will usually be working with other people, so interpersonal and teamworking skills are important. Planning, organisational and time management skills are crucial as you may have to work to high-pressure deadlines, with a lot of work to complete within a short timescale, and will often be working on several tasks simultaneously. As work with IT systems often involves problem-solving, this is another skill that employers value highly. Problem-solving is a skill which combines technical knowledge, experience and a logical approach, and although you won't initially have much experience, having the right approach is half the battle.

On top of these skills, there are a number of more general attributes which all employers will look for, such as dependability, ability to work independently, integrity, confidence and self-motivation.

Which of the skills discussed in this section do you feel most comfortable with and which do you need to improve?

Step One: Understand your course and how it works

Case study: Understanding how a BTEC National course works

Nadia is studying on the BTEC National in IT course at a college in North London. 'To be honest,' she says, 'I knew very little about the course at the start. I had told my careers advisor at school that I wanted to work as a web page developer and he suggested that I went to a college. I applied to a couple of colleges and at the interview they recommended this course. They did tell me a bit about the course at the interview but I don't remember much of it. When I started in September I found it all very confusing. We had an induction but I was really more interested in making friends. I didn't really understand about the difference between the award and the certificate, what credit points are and which units are mandatory. Unlike me, some of my friends on the course did a BTEC First last year so they already understand the way BTEC courses work. It's been a bit harder

for me to get used to everything BTEC but I am now starting to understand it all and am enjoying my course.'

Are you completely new to BTEC like Nadia, or have you studied on a BTEC course before?

If, like Nadia, this is your first BTEC course then the terminology and details of how the course works can be confusing. If this sounds familiar, pay particularly close attention to this step of the Study Guide – it will help you to get up to speed. However, even if you have done a BTEC course before, you should still read this step carefully as not all BTEC courses are the same.

Reflection point

What could Nadia have done to make sure she was better prepared for her new course?

All BTEC Level 3 National qualifications are **vocational** or **work-related**. This means that you gain specific knowledge and understanding relevant to your chosen area. It gives you several advantages when you start work.

For example, you will already know quite a lot about your chosen area, which will help you settle down more quickly. If you are already employed, you become more valuable to your employer.

Activity: Your future options

At the beginning of your new course, it is helpful to think about what options may be available to you for your career pathway in the IT sector. All the assignments on the programme contribute to your final grade and knowing what you are aiming for will help to keep you motivated.

Using a mind map to explore different ideas is a good way to consider the range of options available to you. You will also be able to find out the requirements for each career pathway. For example, if you wish to work in **software development**, you could explore the different routes to becoming a **web programmer**.

You will find the internet a useful source of information. A good starting point is the **'theitjob'** website. Go to page 96 to find out how to access this website.

Your BTEC course will prepare you for the work you want to do.

There are four types of BTEC Level 3 National qualification: Certificates, Subsidiary Diplomas, Diplomas and Extended Diplomas

	Certificate	Subsidiary Diploma	Diploma	Extended Diploma
Credit	30	60	120	180
Equivalence	1 AS-level	1 A-level	2 A-levels	3 A-levels

These qualifications are often described as **nested**. This means that they fit inside each other (rather like Russian dolls) because the same units are common to each qualification – so you can progress from one to another easily by completing more units.

TOP TIP

The structure of BTEC Level 3 National qualifications means it's easy to progress from one type to another and gain more credits, as well as specialise in particular areas that interest you.

- Every BTEC Level 3 National qualification has a set number of **mandatory units** that all learners must complete.
- All BTEC Level 3 National qualifications include **optional units** that enable you to study particular areas in more depth.

- Some BTEC Level 3 National qualifications have **specialist pathways**, which may have additional mandatory units. These specialist pathways allow you to follow your career aims more precisely. For example, if you are studying to become an IT practitioner, you can choose pathways in Software Development, Networking, Systems Support or IT and Business.
- On all BTEC courses you are expected to be responsible for your own learning. Obviously your tutor will give you help and guidance when necessary but you also need to be 'self-starting' and able to use your own initiative. Ideally, you can also assess how well you are doing and make improvements when necessary.
- BTEC Level 3 National grades convert to UCAS points, just like A-levels, but the way you are assessed and graded on a BTEC course is different, as you will see in the next section.

Key points

- You can study part-time or full-time for your BTEC Level 3 National.
- You can do a Certificate, Subsidiary Diploma, Diploma, or Extended Diploma, and progress easily from one to the other.
- You will study both mandatory units and optional units on your course.
- When you have completed your BTEC course you can get a job (or **apprenticeship**), use your qualification to develop your career and/or continue studying to degree level.
- On all BTEC Level 3 National courses, the majority of your learning is practical and vocationally focused to develop the skills you need for your chosen career.

Using the Edexcel website to find out about your course

- You can check all the details about your BTEC Level 3 National course on the Edexcel website – go to www.edexcel.com.
- Enter the BTEC Level 3 National qualification title in the qualifications finder.
- Now find the specification in the list of documents. This is a long document so don't try to print it. Instead, look at the information on the units you will be studying to see the main topics you will cover.
- Then save the document or bookmark the page so that you can easily refer to it again if you need to.

Action points

1 By discussing with your tutor and by exploring the Edexcel website, find out the key information about your course and use it to complete the 'Important Information' form on the next page. You can refer to this form at any time to refresh your memory about any part of your studies.

a) Check whether you are studying for a BTEC Level 3 Certificate, Subsidiary Diploma, Diploma, or Extended Diploma and the number of units you will be studying.

b) Find out the titles of the mandatory units you will be studying.

c) Find out the titles of the optional units and identify the ones offered at your centre.

d) Check the length of your course, and when you will be studying each unit.

e) Identify the optional units you will be taking. On some National courses you will do this at the start, while on others you may make your final decision later.

f) Find out other relevant information about your BTEC Level 3 National qualification. Your centre may have already given you details about the structure.

g) Ask your tutor to help you to complete point 10 on the form. Depending on your course, you may be developing specific additional or personal skills – such as personal, learning and thinking skills (PLTS) and functional skills – or spending time on work experience, going on visits or doing other activities linked to your subject area.

h) Talk to your tutor about point 12 on the form as your sources of information will depend on the careers guidance and information at your centre. You may find it useful to exchange ideas with other members of your class.

IMPORTANT INFORMATION ON MY BTEC LEVEL 3 NATIONAL COURSE	
1	The title of the BTEC Level 3 National qualification I am studying is:
2	The length of my course is:
3	The total number of units I will study is:
4	The number of mandatory units I have to study is:
5	The titles of these mandatory units and the dates (or terms) when I will study them are:
6	The main topics I will learn in each mandatory unit include:

IMPORTANT INFORMATION ON MY BTEC LEVEL 3 NATIONAL COURSE	
7	The number of optional units I have to study is:
8	The titles of the optional units I will study are:
9	The main topics I will learn in each optional unit include:
10	Other important aspects of my course are:
11	After I have achieved my BTEC Level 3 National my options include:
12	Useful sources of information I can use to find out more about these options include:

2 Many learners already have information, contacts or direct experiences that relate to their course. For example, you may have a specific interest or hobby that links to a unit, such as being a St John Ambulance cadet if you are studying Public Services. Think about the relevant sources of information you already have access to and complete the table below.

MY INFORMATION SOURCES	
Experts I know	(Who they are, what they know)
My hobbies and interests	(What they are, what they involve)
My job(s)	(Past and present work and work experience, and what I did)
Programmes I like to watch	(What these are, how they relate to my course)
Magazines and/or books I read	(What these are, examples of relevant articles)
ICT sources	(My centre's intranet as well as useful websites)
Other	(Other sources relevant for my particular course and the topics I will be studying)

Step Two: Understand how you are assessed and graded

Case study: Thinking about assessment

Ethan is just starting the second year of his BTEC National Diploma.

'During my first year I didn't really put a lot of effort into my work as I thought it would be fine to just get Pass grades. After all, as long as you pass a course that's fine, isn't it?'

However Ethan has now discovered a problem.

'I really want to go to university next year to study Computer Science with a focus on programming and robotics, so I have to start doing my UCAS application soon. I have started to research various different universities and the courses I am interested in, but I am finding that many of the ones that I like the sound of and have the most interesting programming modules want higher grades. Having got mostly Pass grades on the units I did in the first year it's now going to be really hard to push my overall grade up to the Merits or Distinctions that they

want. Also, the fact that I only got a Pass for my first year Principles of Software Design and Development unit is really going to hold me back.'

Ethan now regrets cruising in the first year and realises that if he had looked into this earlier he would have done things differently.

Reflection point

Do you have a specific career in mind or an interest in a particular area of IT? If one or more of the units you are studying relates to that career or interest then it is important to get good grades in that unit/those units. Otherwise, it may be very hard to explain at a job or university interview why you don't have good grades in the subject that relates to the job or course you are applying for!

Your assessment

This section looks at the importance of your assignments, how they are graded and how this converts into unit points and UCAS points. Unlike A-levels, there are no externally-set final exams on a BTEC course. Even if you know this because you already have a BTEC First qualification, you should still read this section as now you will be working at a different level.

Your learning is assessed by **assignments**, set by your tutors. You will complete these throughout

your course, using many different **assessment methods**, such as real-life case studies, **projects** and presentations. Some assignments may be work-based or **time-constrained** – it depends very much on the vocational area you are studying.

Your assignments are based on **learning outcomes** set by Edexcel. These are listed for each unit in your course specification. You must achieve **all** the learning outcomes to pass each unit.

Important skills to help you achieve your grades include:

- researching and analysing information (see page 63)
- using your time effectively (see page 23)
- working co-operatively as a member of a team (see page 57).

Your grades, unit points and UCAS points

On a BTEC Level 3 National course, assessments that meet the learning outcomes are graded as pass, merit or distinction. The different grades within each unit are set out by Edexcel as **grading criteria** in a **grading grid**. These criteria identify the **higher-level skills** you must demonstrate to achieve a higher grade (see also Step Six – Understand your assessment, on page 33).

All your assessment grades earn **unit points**. The total points you get for all your units determines your final qualification grade(s) – pass, merit or distinction. You get:

- one final grade if you are taking a Certificate or Subsidiary Diploma
- two final grades if you are taking a Diploma
- three final grades if you are taking an Extended Diploma.

Your points and overall grade(s) convert to **UCAS points**, which you need to be accepted onto a degree course. For example, if you achieve three final pass grades for your BTEC Level 3 Extended Diploma, you get 120 UCAS Tariff points. If you achieve three final distinction grades, this increases to 360 – equivalent to three GCE A-levels.

Please note that all UCAS information was correct at the time of going to print, but we would advise you to check their website for the most up to date information. See page 96 for how to access their website.

Case study: Securing a university place

Chris and Shaheeda both want a university place and have worked hard on their BTEC Level 3 Extended Diploma course.

Chris's final score is 226 unit points, which converts to 280 UCAS Tariff points. Shaheeda has a total score of 228 unit points – just two points more – which converts to 320 UCAS points! This is because a score of between 204 and 227 unit points gives 280 UCAS points, whereas a score of 228 to 251 points gives 320 UCAS points.

Shaheeda is delighted because this increases her chances of getting a place on the degree course she wants. Chris is annoyed. He says if he had realised he would have worked harder on his last assignment to get two points more.

You start to earn points from your first assessment, so you get many benefits from settling in quickly and doing good work from the start. Understanding how **grade boundaries** work also helps you to focus your efforts to get the best possible final grade.

You will be able to discuss your learning experiences, your personal progress and the achievement of your learning objectives in **individual tutorials** with your tutor. These enable you to monitor your progress and overcome temporary difficulties. You can also talk about any worries you have. Your tutor is one of your most important resources and a tutorial gives you their undivided attention.

You can talk through any questions or problems in your tutorials.

Key points

- Your learning is assessed in a variety of ways, such as by assignments, projects and real-life case studies.
- You need to demonstrate specific knowledge and skills to achieve the learning outcomes set by Edexcel. You must achieve all the grading criteria to pass a unit.
- The grading criteria for pass, merit and distinction are shown in a grading grid for the unit. Higher-level skills are needed for higher grades.
- The assessment grades of pass, merit and distinction convert to unit points. The total unit points you receive for the course determines your final overall grade(s) and UCAS points.

TOP TIP

It's always tempting to spend longer on work you like doing and are good at, but focusing on improving your weak areas will do more to boost your overall grade(s).

Action points

1 Find out more about your own course by carrying out this activity.

a) Find the learning outcomes for the units you are currently studying. Your tutor may have given you these, or you can find them in your course specification – go to www.edexcel.com.

b) Look at the grading grid for the units and identify the way the requirements change for the higher grades. If there are some unfamiliar words, check these in Step Six of this guide (see page 33 onwards).

c) If the unit points system still seems complicated, ask your tutor to explain it.

d) Check the UCAS points you would need for the course or university which interests you.

e) Design a form you can use to record the unit points you earn throughout your course. Keep this up-to-date. Regularly check how your points relate to your overall grade(s), based on the grade boundaries for your qualification. Your tutor can give you this information or you can check it yourself in the course specification.

Activity: Tracking your progress

What units are you doing this year on your course? Have you thought about how you will track your progress as you complete assignments and see which grade you are on course to achieve? Try creating a grading progress sheet to monitor how well you are doing in each unit. Look at the specification (you can download this from the Edexcel website www.edexcel.com) and find the grading criteria for each unit. Most units have about six or seven Pass criteria, two or three Merit criteria and one or two Distinction criteria. List the grading criteria for each unit on your progress sheet. As you complete your assignments you can tick off the criteria you have achieved and see your overall progress. Your grading progress sheet might look like this:

Unit 1	Communication and Employability Skills for IT									
Pass Criteria						Merit			Distinction	
P1	P2	P3	P4	P5	P6	M1	M2	M3	D1	D2
✓		✓				✓				

Unit 2	Computer Systems										
Pass Criteria								Merit			Distinction
P1	P2	P3	P4	P5	P6	P7	P8	M1	M2	M3	D1	D2
✓		✓		✓					✓			

Rather than using a form to record your grades you could use a spreadsheet instead. You could create quite a sophisticated spreadsheet which will automatically show your grade points and overall grades as you complete your assignments. However, you will need to test it carefully to check that the results it gives you are correct.

Step Three: Understand yourself

Case study: Becoming self-aware

Matt didn't do too well with his GCSEs as he found exams very difficult and he left school feeling that education wasn't really for him. His mum persuaded him to go to college but he didn't enjoy the Business course he enrolled on and felt like he needed to do something more practical. He left the course after 3 months and got a job working in a burger bar, but he hated that too and felt like a failure in a dead end job. He spoke to his family and the 'Connexions' advisor at his old college and they helped him decide what he should be doing. He told them about his interest in computers and that he was thinking of a career in that area. They identified that he needed a course that was less academic, had more focus on practical activities and didn't involve examinations.

The next September he enrolled on a BTEC First in IT. This time he was determined to complete the course and, although he found it hard going at times, he was successful and completed the course with a Merit. Now studying the first year of his BTEC National in IT, he feels more positive. 'I didn't enjoy school,' he says. 'There were too many subjects and I don't get on well with exams. Also I find all that theory very boring. I'm the sort of person who likes doing things, not just listening or reading. The BTEC approach is more to my liking. There is still quite a lot of theory, which I'm not crazy about, but I'm coping and I really enjoying the practical elements.' Matt has developed an interest in software development, something he would never have thought of before, and in the second year of his BTEC he plans to choose optional units related to programming.

Reflection point

How do your think your personality and interests are suited to a BTEC course?

Self-awareness means understanding how you 'tick'. For example, do you prefer practical activities rather than theory? Do you prefer to draw or sketch an idea, rather than write about it?

Self-awareness is important as it makes you less reliant on other people's opinions and gives you confidence in your own judgement. You can also reflect on your actions to learn from your experiences.

Self-awareness also means knowing your own strengths and weaknesses. Knowing your strengths enables you to feel positive and confident about yourself and your abilities. Knowing your weaknesses means you know the areas you need to develop.

You can analyse yourself by looking at...

... your personality and preferences

You may have taken a personality test at your centre. If not, your tutor may recommend one to use, or there are many available online.

Many employers ask job candidates to complete a personality test so that they can match the type of work they are offering to the most suitable candidates. Although these tests can only give a broad indication of someone's personality they may help to avoid mismatches, such as hiring someone who is introverted to work in sales.

... your skills and abilities

To succeed in your assignments, and to progress in a career, requires a number of skills. Some may be vocationally specific, or professional, skills that you can improve during your course – such as sporting performance on a Sports course. Others are broader skills that are invaluable no matter what you are studying – such as communicating clearly and co-operating with others.

You will work faster and more accurately, and have greater confidence, if you are skilled and proficient. A quick skills check will identify any problem areas.

TOP TIP

Use the Skills Building section on page 85 to identify the skills you need for your course. You'll also find hints and tips for improving any weak areas.

Key points

- You need certain skills and abilities to get the most out of your BTEC Level 3 National course and to develop your career potential.
- Knowing your strengths and weaknesses is a sign of maturity. It gives you greater confidence in your abilities and enables you to focus on areas for improvement.

TOP TIP

You will find more help on developing your skills and abilities in the sections on: Working as a member of a group; Using time wisely; Researching and analysing information; and Making effective presentations.

Action points

1 Gain insight into your own personality by answering each of the following statements **True** or **False** with a tick. Be honest!

		True	False
a)	If someone annoys me, I can tell them about it without causing offence.		
b)	If someone is talking, I often interrupt them to give them my opinion.		
c)	I get really stressed if I'm under pressure.		
d)	I can sometimes become very emotional and upset on other people's behalf.		
e)	I sometimes worry that I can't cope and may make a mess of something.		
f)	I am usually keen, enthusiastic and motivated to do well.		
g)	I enjoy planning and organising my work.		
h)	I find it easy to work and co-operate with other people and take account of their opinions.		
i)	I am easily influenced by other people.		
j)	I often jump to conclusions and judge people and situations on first impressions.		
k)	I prefer to rely on facts and experience rather than following my instincts.		

Now identify which of the skills and qualities in the box below will be really important in your chosen career.

> tact   truthfulness   listening skills
>
> **staying calm under pressure**
>
> **empathy with others**   self-confidence
>
> initiative   planning and organising
>
> **working with others**   self-assurance
>
> **objective judgements**

Use your answers to identify areas you should work on to be successful in the future.

2 As part of the UCAS process, all **higher education** applicants have to write a personal statement. This is different from a CV, which is a summary of achievements that all job applicants prepare. You may have already prepared a CV but not thought about a personal statement. Now is your chance to!

Read the information about personal statements in the box. Then answer these questions:

a) Explain why personal statements are so important for higher education applicants.

b) Why do you think it is important for your personal statement to read well and be error-free?

c) Suggest three reasons why you shouldn't copy a pre-written statement you have found online.

d) Check websites about personal statements to see what to include in the statement and how to set it out. Go to page 96 to find out how to access helpful websites.

e) Prepare a bullet point list of ten personal facts. Focus on your strengths and good reasons why you should be given a place on the higher education course of your choice. If possible, discuss your list with your tutor. Then keep it safely, as it will be useful if you need to write a personal statement later.

Personal statements

This is the information that all higher education applicants have to put in the blank space on their UCAS form. The aim is to sell yourself to admissions tutors. It can be pretty scary, especially if you haven't written anything like it before.

So, where do you start?

First, **never** copy pre-written statements you find online. These are just for guidance. Even worse are websites that offer to write your statement for a fee, and send you a few general, pre-written paragraphs. Forget them all: you can do better!

Imagine you are an admissions tutor with 60 places to offer to 200 applicants. What will you need to read in a personal statement to persuade you to offer the applicant a place?

Most likely, clear explanations about:

* what the applicant can contribute to the course
* why the applicant really wants a place on your course
* what the applicant has done to further his or her own interests in this area, eg voluntary work
* attributes that show this applicant would be a definite bonus – such as innovative ideas, with evidence eg 'I organised a newsletter which we published every three months …'

A personal statement should be well written, with no grammatical or spelling errors and organised into clear paragraphs.

For further guidance, go to page 96 to find out how to access a number of helpful websites.

Activity: Strengths and areas for improvement

IT employers and universities expect candidates to be able to demonstrate their attributes – from personal statements to job applications, this is an important skill.

Use the table below to identify your strengths and areas for development with regard to the attributes listed. You should also consider how you can demonstrate these attributes to prospective employers and/or on your UCAS personal statement.

Attribute	Strengths	How can I improve?	How I can demonstrate this?
Technical knowledge (example)	*Excellent knowledge of Windows XP, especially network configuration. Also very good knowledge of PC hardware installation and troubleshooting*	*Read latest magazine articles, get as much practice as possible doing installations and troubleshooting. Improve knowledge of Windows 7*	*By getting Distinction grades in the Computer Systems and other hardware-related units.* *Maybe through a related work placement*
Technical knowledge			
Customer service skills			
Numeracy and Literacy			
Interpersonal skills			
Teamworking			
Planning and organising			
Time management			
Problem solving			

Step Four: Use your time wisely

Case study: Time management

It's an important week for Vijay. He has two assignments to complete by Friday. He plans to make some progress on them over the weekend, then finish them off during the week.

On Saturday he works at a local electrical superstore and goes out in the evening. Sunday morning is a chance to lie in but he plans to work on his assignments in the afternoon. However at 10 am his mum wakes him. His boss from the superstore is on the phone, begging him to come in as several people with flu have left him short staffed. Vijay really doesn't want to but double-time pay will come in handy so he drags himself out of bed. 4 pm can't come around fast enough as he feels awful. By the time he gets home at 4.30 he is fit for nothing and collapses in front of the TV for the rest of the evening.

On Monday morning he wakes up late and it's a rush to get to college for his 9 am class. He is committed to working on his assignments in the afternoon but knows that time is now running short. After lunch he goes to the IT workshop to get on with his work. When he gets there he is frustrated to find there are no computers free; everyone needs to get their assignments done. He now faces a dilemma – he could go home to work on his PC but he has football practice at 4.30 so he won't have much time. He waits for 30 minutes or so to see if any computers become free but it's hopeless as the workshop is busier than he has ever seen it.

On Tuesday Vijay wakes up early in a panic. He can't believe he only has 4 days until the assignments must be handed in and he has done nothing! He rushes to college early so he can get one the computers in the workshop before it gets busy. He works non-stop for most of the morning and loses track of time so he is nearly late for his 11 am class. Later on that day he realises he can't find his USB stick. He searches everywhere but there is no sign of it. He really can't believe it – all his work is lost and worst of all he hasn't done a backup since last week so he has lost all his notes and the research he did for the assignment. There are 3 days to go and he is back to square one.

In the end Vijay gets both assignments finished by staying up late to complete them and skipping classes. However he is not happy with them and he knows he could do better.

Reflection point

Vijay made a number of mistakes in his approach to his college work. What do you think he did wrong? How could he have avoided making these mistakes?

Most learners have to combine course commitments with other responsibilities such as a job (either full- or part-time) and family responsibilities. You will also want to see your friends and keep up your hobbies and interests. Juggling these successfully means you need to be able to use your time wisely.

This involves planning what to do and when to do it to prevent panics about unexpected deadlines. As your course progresses, this becomes even more important as your workload may increase towards the end of a term. In some cases there could be two or more assignments to complete simultaneously. Although tutors try to avoid clashes of this sort, it is sometimes inevitable.

To cope successfully, you need time-management skills, in particular:

- how to organise your time to be more productive
- how to prioritise tasks
- how to overcome time-wasters.

Organising your time

- **Use a diary or wall chart.**
  Using a different colour pen for each, enter:
  - your course commitments, eg assignment dates, tutorials, visits
  - important personal commitments, eg sports matches, family birthdays
  - your work commitments.

TOP TIP

A diary is useful because you can update it as you go, but a wall chart gives you a better overview of your commitments over several weeks. Keep your diary or chart up-to-date and check ahead regularly so that you have prior warning of important dates.

- **Identify how you currently use your time.**
  - Work out how much time you spend at your centre, at work, at home and on social activities.
  - Identify which commitments are vital and which are optional so you can find extra time if necessary.

- **Plan and schedule future commitments.**
  - Write down any appointments and tasks you must do.
  - Enter assignment review dates and final deadline dates in different colours.
  - This should stop you from arranging a dental appointment on the same morning that you are due to give an important presentation – or planning a hectic social life when you have lots of course work to do.

- **Decide your best times for doing course work.**
  - Expect to do most of your course work in your own time.
  - Work at the time of day when you feel at your best.
  - Work regularly, and in relatively short bursts, rather than once or twice a week for very long stretches.
  - If you're a night owl, allow an hour to 'switch off' before you go to bed.

- **Decide where to work.**
  - Choose somewhere you can concentrate without interruption.
  - Make sure there is space for resources you use, such as books or specialist equipment.
  - You also need good lighting and a good – but not too comfortable – chair.
  - If you can't find suitable space at home, check out your local or college library.

- **Assemble the items you need.**
  - Book ahead to get specific books, journals or DVDs from the library.
  - Ensure you have your notes, handouts and assignment brief with you.
  - Use sticky notes to mark important pages in textbooks or folders.

TOP TIP

Set yourself a target when you start work, so that you feel positive and productive at the end. Always try to end a session when a task is going well, rather than when you are stuck. Then you will be keener to go back to it the next day. Note down outstanding tasks you need to continue with next time.

- **Plan ahead.**
  - If anything is unclear about an assignment, ask your tutor for an explanation as soon as you can.
  - Break down long tasks or assignments into manageable chunks, eg find information, decide what to use, create a plan for finished work, write rough draft of first section, etc.
  - Work back from deadline dates so that you allow plenty of time to do the work.
  - Always allow more time than you need. It is better to finish early than to run out of time.

TOP TIP

If you are working on a task as a group, organise and agree times to work together. Make sure you have somewhere to meet where you can work without disturbing other courses or groups.

- **Be self-disciplined.**
  - Don't put things off because you're not in the mood. Make it easier by doing simple tasks first to get a sense of achievement. Then move on to something harder.
  - Plan regular breaks. If you're working hard you need a change of activity to recharge your batteries.
  - If you have a serious problem or personal crisis, talk to your personal tutor promptly.

TOP TIP

Make sure you know the consequences of missing an assignment deadline, as well as the dispensations and exemptions that can be given if you have an unavoidable and serious problem, such as illness (see also pages 34 and 83).

How to prioritise tasks

Prioritising means doing the most important and urgent task first. Normally this will be the task or assignment with the closest deadline or the one that will most affect your overall course grades.

One way of prioritising is to group tasks into ABC categories.

Category A tasks	These must be done now as they are very important and cannot be delayed, eg completing an assignment to be handed in tomorrow.
Category B tasks	These are jobs you should do if you have time, because otherwise they will rapidly become Category A, eg getting a book that you need for your next assignment.
Category C tasks	These are tasks you should do if you have the time, eg rewriting notes jotted down quickly in a lesson.

Expect to be flexible. For example, if you need to allow time for information to arrive, then send for this first. If you are working in a team, take into account other people's schedules when you are making arrangements.

BTEC's own resources

Avoiding time-wasters

Everyone has days when they don't know where the time has gone. It may be because they were constantly interrupted or because things just kept going wrong. Whatever the reason, the end result is that some jobs don't get done.

If this happens to you regularly, you need to take steps to keep on track.

Some useful tips are:

- **Warn people in advance when you will be working.**
  - Ask them to not interrupt you.
  - If you are in a separate room, shut the door. If someone comes in, make it clear you don't want to talk.
  - If that doesn't work, find somewhere else (or some other time) to work.
- **Switch off your mobile, TV, radio and iPod/MP3 player.**
  - Don't respond to, or make, calls or texts.
  - If someone rings your home phone, let voicemail answer or ask them to call back later.
- **Be strict with yourself when you are working online.**
  - Don't check your email until you've finished work.
  - Don't get distracted when searching for information.
  - Keep away from social networking sites.
- **Avoid displacement activities.**
  - These are the normally tedious jobs, such as cleaning your computer screen, that suddenly seem far more attractive than working!

Talking to friends can occupy a lot of time.

TOP TIP

The first step in managing your own time is learning to say 'no' (nicely!) if someone asks you to do something tempting when you should be working.

Key points

- Being in control of your time allows you to balance your commitments according to their importance and means you won't let anyone down.
- Organising yourself and your time involves knowing how you spend your time now, planning when and where it is best to work, scheduling commitments and setting sensible timescales to complete your work.
- Knowing how to prioritise means you will schedule work effectively according to its urgency and importance. You will need self-discipline to follow the schedule you have set for yourself.
- Identifying ways in which you may waste time means you can guard against these to achieve your goals more easily.

TOP TIP

Benefits to managing your own time include being less stressed (because you are not reacting to problems or crises), producing better work and having time for a social life.

Action points

1 Start planning your time properly.

a) Find out how many assignments you will have this term, and when you will get them. Put this information into your diary or planner.

b) Update this with your other commitments for the term – both work/course-related and social. Identify possible clashes and decide how to resolve the problem.

c) Identify one major task or assignment you will do soon. Divide it into manageable chunks and decide how long to allow for each chunk, plus some spare time for any problems. If possible, check your ideas with your tutor before you put them into your planner.

2 How good are you at being responsible for your own learning?

a) Fill in the following table. Score yourself out of 5 for each area: where 0 is awful and 5 is excellent. Ask a friend or relative to score you as well. See if you can explain any differences.

	Scoring yourself	Other person's score for you
Being punctual		
Organisational ability		
Tidiness		
Working accurately		
Finding and correcting own mistakes		
Solving problems		
Accepting responsibility		
Working with details		
Planning how to do a job		
Using own initiative		
Thinking up new ideas		
Meeting deadlines		

b) Draw up your own action plan for areas where you need to improve. If possible, talk this through at your next **tutorial** (see page 16).

Activity: Organising your time

You may find it helpful to use computer systems to help you allocate your time and remind you of important events. Most mobile phones (especially 'smartphones' such as the Apple iPhone) have calendars where you can allocate times and set reminders. The same is true of many web-based email systems, such as Google mail, and some will even synchronise with your phone. Many systems also provide a 'to do' list where you can list outstanding tasks.

1. Investigate what calendar systems are available on your phone and by your email provider and select one to use (you may need to try out several to see which one suits you best).

2. Put all your assignment deadline dates into your calendar and add a reminder one week before the due date so that you have plenty of time to get everything ready to hand in.

3. Set a weekly reminder to back up your USB memory stick.

4. Make use of a 'to do' list to keep track of all your outstanding tasks. Add new ones as they occur (e.g. 'complete homework for Unit 1') and tick them off as they are done.

5. To get you thinking about how to organise your week, complete the timetable below with all your lessons. Allocate self-study periods each week and add these to the timetable calendar. Add other non-course-related commitments, such as part-time work, weekly sports practice, etc. You could then put this information onto a computer system if you find that this helps you remember when you need to do things.

Day	Monday	Tuesday	Wednesday	Thursday	Friday	Saturday	Sunday
9–11							
11–1							
1–3							
3-6							
Evening							

TOP TIP

Don't waste time doing things that distract you when studying for this course. In the business, time costs money.

Step Five: Utilise all your resources

Case study: Finding suitable resources

Sally is working on an assignment for Unit 4: Impact of the Use of IT on Business Systems and she needs to find some information about how IT developments affect businesses. She searches on the internet but can't find very much information on this topic, and what she does find is quite complex and difficult to understand.

She works at her local supermarket on a Saturday and decides to ask her boss if he has any ideas. He gives her the phone number of a manager in the IT department and she gives him a ring. He is very helpful; he gives her some good ideas and emails her some useful information.

Sally also visits her local library and finds several books that look quite useful. However, when she reads the relevant sections in the books she finds that the information seems quite dated. She checks when the books were published and discovers they are from the 1990s, so she does not think this information is very useful. On the other hand, she has been in the habit of checking newspapers and magazines for relevant articles and has collected a couple which are relevant to this unit.

Sally also speaks to her uncle. He has been working in a bank for many years so she asks him what changes computers have made to his job. He gives her some ideas about how internet banking in particular has had a big impact on how banks do business and also mentions how security issues have become a big headache for banks, with hackers and fraudsters stealing millions every year.

Reflection points

What do you think is meant by the term 'resource'?

What range of different resources could you use to collect information?

Your resources are all the things that can help you to be successful in your BTEC Level 3 National qualification, from your favourite website to your **study buddy** (see page 30) who collects handouts for you if you miss a class.

Your centre will provide essential resources, such as a library with appropriate books and electronic reference sources, the computer network and internet access. You will have to provide basic resources such as pens, pencils and file folders yourself. If you have to buy your own textbooks, look after them carefully so you can sell them on at the end of your course.

Here is a list of resources, with tips for getting the best out of them.

- **Course information**. This includes your course specification, this Study Skills Guide and all information on the Edexcel website relating to your BTEC Level 3 National course. Course information from your centre will include term dates, assignment dates and your timetable. Keep everything safely so you can refer to it whenever you need to clarify something.

- **Course materials**. These include course handouts, printouts, your own notes and textbooks. Put handouts into an A4 folder as soon as you get them. Use a separate folder for each unit you study.

TOP TIP

Filing notes and handouts promptly means they don't get lost, will stay clean and uncrumpled and you won't waste time looking for them.

- **Stationery**. You need pens and pencils, a notepad, a hole puncher, a stapler and sets of dividers. Dividers should be clearly labelled to help you store and quickly find notes, printouts and handouts. Your notes should be headed and dated, and those from your own research must also include your source (see Step Eight – page 63 onwards).

- **People**. Your tutors, specialist staff at college, classmates, your employer and work colleagues, your relatives and friends are all valuable resources. Many will have particular skills or work in the vocational area that you are studying. Talking to other learners can help to clarify issues that there may not have been time to discuss fully in class.

  A **study buddy** is another useful resource as they can make notes and collect handouts if you miss a session. (Remember to return the favour when they are away.)

Always be polite when you are asking people for information. Prepare the questions first and remember that you are asking for help, not trying to get them to do the work for you! If you are interviewing someone for an assignment or project, good preparations are vital. (See Step Eight – page 63 onwards.)

If someone who did the course before you offers help, be careful. It is likely the course requirements will have changed. Never be tempted to copy their assignments (or someone else's). This is **plagiarism** – a deadly sin in the educational world (see also Step Six – page 33).

TOP TIP

A positive attitude, an enquiring mind and the ability to focus on what is important will have a major impact on your final result.

Key points

- Resources help you to achieve your qualification. Find out what resources you have available to you and use them wisely.

- Have your own stationery items.

- Know how to use central facilities and resources such as the library, learning resource centres and your computer network. Always keep to the policy on IT use in your centre.

- People are a key resource – school or college staff, work colleagues, members of your class, friends, family and people who are experts in their field.

Action points

1 a) List the resources you will need to complete your course successfully. Identify which ones will be provided by your school or college, and which you need to supply yourself.

b) Go through your list again and identify the resources you already have (or know how to access) and those you don't.

c) Compare your list with a friend's and decide how to obtain and access the resources you need. Add any items to your list that you forgot.

d) List the items you still need to get and set a target date for doing this.

2 'Study buddy' schemes operate in many centres. Find out if this applies to your own centre and how you can make the best use of it.

In some you can choose your study buddy, in others people are paired up by their tutor.

- Being a study buddy might mean just collecting handouts when the other person is absent, and giving them important news.
- It may also mean studying together and meeting (or keeping contact by phone or email) to exchange ideas and share resources.

With a study buddy you can share resources and stay on top of the course if you're ever away.

Activity: Using resources

Unit 2: Computer Systems is mandatory and requires you to recommend a computer system for a specified business purpose (i.e. not just home use).

Look at these potential business computer users and list the different ways in which they could make use of a computer.

Potential business computer user	How they could make use of a computer
A shopkeeper who runs a small hardware store	
A photographer who shoots weddings, portraits, family groups, etc.	
A plumbing company that employs five plumbers who visit private homes to fix plumbing problems	
A home tutoring company that arranges tutors to visit children at home to give additional classes in Maths, English, etc.	

Having looked at possible uses for a computer in these different businesses, you will need to research suitable computers and software. Use the table below to list the actual resources you could use to do this.

Internet websites

Magazines

Shops (check in Yellow Pages for computer shops in your area)

Step Six: Understand your assessment

📁 Case study: The first assignment

Kalid was new to BTEC when he started his course. He was a bit worried about his first assignment as he wanted to do well, but when he read the brief his teacher gave him it all seemed fairly simple. He started to work on it and although his teacher told the class to bring drafts to show him how they were doing, Kalid didn't really see the point. He put a lot of work into it but ran out of time towards the deadline which meant he didn't do as much as he would have liked on the last couple of tasks. Nevertheless he managed to hand the assignment in on time. It was a real disappointment to have it returned a week later and find he had only achieved the Pass criteria. He had really hoped the work he had done was good enough for at least a Merit.

When Khalid discussed the assignment with his teacher it was clear he had made a mistake. The assignment had been split up into various tasks, each of which covered a different grading criteria, but Khalid had failed to notice this. The first two tasks, which he had focused on, covered Pass criteria and he had done more work on these than was necessary. The other two tasks covered Merit and Distinction criteria but Khalid had run out of time to work on these, and what he had done was not sufficient to achieve the higher grades.

Reflection point

How can Khalid avoid making the same mistake again?

Being successful on any BTEC Level 3 National course means first understanding what you must do in your assignments – and then doing it.

Your assignments focus on topics you have already covered in class. If you've attended regularly, you should be able to complete them confidently.

However, there are some common pitfalls it's worth thinking about. Here are tips to avoid them:

- Read the instructions (the assignment brief) properly and several times before you start.
- Make sure you understand what you are supposed to do. Ask if anything is unclear.

- Complete every part of a task. If you ignore a question, you can't meet the grading criteria.
- Prepare properly. Do your research or reading before you start. Don't guess the answers.
- Communicate your ideas clearly. You can check this by asking someone who doesn't know the subject to look at your work.
- Only include relevant information. Padding out answers makes it look as if you don't know your subject.
- Do the work earlier rather than later to avoid any last-minute panics.
- Pay attention to advice and feedback that your tutor has given you.

The assignment 'brief'

This may be longer than its name implies! The assignment brief includes all the instructions for an assignment and several other details, as you can see in the table below.

What will you find in a BTEC Level 3 National assignment brief?	
Content	Details
Title	This will link to the unit and learning outcomes
Format/style	Written assignment, presentation, demonstration, etc
Preparation	Read case study, do research, etc
Learning outcomes	These state the knowledge you must demonstrate to obtain a required grade
Grading criterion/ criteria covered	eg P1/M1/D1
Individual/group work	Remember to identify your own contribution in any group work
Feedback	Tutor, peer review
Interim review dates	Dates to see your tutor
Final deadline	Last submission date

Your centre's rules and regulations

Your centre will have several policies and guidelines about assignments, which you need to check carefully. Many, such as those listed below, relate to Edexcel policies and guidelines.

- The procedure to follow if you have a serious problem and can't meet a deadline. An extension may be granted.
- The penalty for missing a deadline without good reason.
- The penalty for copying someone else's work. This is usually severe, so never share your work (or CDs or USB flash drive) with anyone else, and don't borrow theirs.
- **Plagiarism** is also serious misconduct. This means copying someone's work or quoting from books and websites and pretending it is your own work.
- The procedure to follow if you disagree with the grade you are given.

Understanding the question or task

There are two aspects to a question or task. The first is the **command words**, which are described below. The second is the **presentation instructions**, which is what you are asked to do – don't write a report when you should be producing a chart!

Command words, such as 'explain', 'describe', 'analyse' and 'evaluate' state how a question must be answered. You may be asked to 'describe' something at pass level, but you will need to do more, perhaps 'analyse' or 'evaluate', to achieve merit or distinction.

Many learners fail to achieve higher grades because they don't realise the difference between these words. Instead of analysing or evaluating they give an explanation instead. Adding more details won't achieve a higher grade – you need to change your whole approach to the answer.

The **grading grid** for each unit of your course gives you the command words, so that you know what to do to achieve a pass, merit or distinction. The tables that follow show you what is usually required when you see a particular command word. These are just examples to guide you as the exact response will depend on the question. If you have any doubts, check with your tutor before you start work.

There are two important points to note.

- A command word, such as 'create' or 'explain', may be repeated in the grading criteria for different grades. In these cases the complexity or range of the task itself increases at the higher grades.
- Command words vary depending on your vocational area. So Art and Design grading grids may use different command words from Applied Science, for example.

TOP TIP

Look at this section again when you get your first assignment and check the command words against these explanations.

To obtain a pass grade

To achieve a pass you must usually demonstrate that you understand the important facts relating to a topic and can state these clearly and concisely.

Command words for a pass	Meaning
Create (or produce)	Make, invent or construct an item.
Describe	Give a clear, straightforward description that includes all the main points and links these together logically.
Define	Clearly explain what a particular term means and give an example, if appropriate, to show what you mean.
Explain … how/why	Set out in detail the meaning of something, with reasons. It is often helpful to give an example of what you mean. Start with the topic then give the 'how' or 'why'.
Identify	Distinguish and state the main features or basic facts relating to a topic.
Interpret	Define or explain the meaning of something.
Illustrate	Give examples to show what you mean.
List	Provide the information required in a list rather than in continuous writing.
Outline	Write a clear description that includes all the main points but avoid going into too much detail.
Plan (or devise)	Work out and explain how you would carry out a task or activity.
Select (and present) information	Identify relevant information to support the argument you are making and communicate this in an appropriate way.
State	Write a clear and full account.
Undertake	Carry out a specific activity.
Examples:	
Identify the main features on a digital camera.	
Outline the steps to take to carry out research for an assignment.	

To obtain a merit grade

To obtain a merit you must prove that you can apply your knowledge in a specific way.

Command words for a merit	Meaning
Analyse	Identify separate factors, say how they relate to each other and how each one relates to the topic.
Classify	Sort your information into appropriate categories before presenting or explaining it.
Compare and contrast	Identify the main factors that apply in two or more situations and explain the similarities and differences or advantages and disadvantages.
Demonstrate	Provide several relevant examples or appropriate evidence which support the arguments you are making. In some vocational areas this may also mean giving a practical performance.
Discuss	Provide a thoughtful and logical argument to support the case you are making.
Explain (in detail)	Provide details and give reasons and/or evidence to clearly support the argument you are making.
Implement	Put into practice or operation. You may also have to interpret or justify the effect or result.
Interpret	Understand and explain an effect or result.
Justify	Give appropriate reasons to support your opinion or views and show how you arrived at these conclusions.
Relate/report	Give a full account, with reasons.
Research	Carry out a full investigation.
Specify	Provide full details and descriptions of selected items or activities.
Examples: Compare and contrast the performance of two different digital cameras. Explain in detail the steps to take to research an assignment.	

To obtain a distinction grade

To obtain a distinction you must prove that you can make a reasoned judgement based on appropriate evidence.

Command words for a distinction	Meaning
Analyse	Identify the key factors, show how they are linked and explain the importance and relevance of each.
Assess	Give careful consideration to all the factors or events that apply and identify which are the most important and relevant, with reasons.
Comprehensively explain	Give a very detailed explanation that covers all the relevant points and give reasons for your views or actions.
Critically comment	Give your view after you have considered all the evidence, particularly the importance of both the relevant positive and negative aspects.
Evaluate	Review the information and then bring it together to form a conclusion. Give evidence to support each of your views or statements.
Evaluate critically	Review the information to decide the degree to which something is true, important or valuable. Then assess possible alternatives, taking into account their strengths and weaknesses if they were applied instead. Then give a precise and detailed account to explain your opinion.
Summarise	Identify/review the main, relevant factors and/or arguments so that these are explained in a clear and concise manner.
Examples: Assess ten features commonly found on a digital camera. Analyse your own ability to carry out effective research for an assignment.	

TOP TIP

Check that you understand *exactly* how to demonstrate each of the learning outcomes specified in the assignment.

Responding positively

Assignments enable you to demonstrate what you know and how you can apply it. You should respond positively to the challenge and give it your best shot. Being well organised and having confidence in your own abilities helps too, and this is covered in the next section.

Key points

- Read instructions carefully so that you don't make mistakes that can easily be avoided, such as only doing part of the set task.
- Note the assignment deadline on your planner and any interim review dates. Schedule work around these dates to make the most of reviews with your tutor.
- Check your centre's policies relating to assignments, such as how to obtain an extension or query a final grade.
- Expect command words and/or the complexity of a task to be different at higher grades, because you have to demonstrate higher-level skills.

TOP TIP

All your assignments will relate to topics you have covered and work you have done in class. They're not meant to be a test to catch you out.

Action points

1 Check your ability to differentiate between different types of command words by doing this activity.
   a) Prepare a brief description of your usual lifestyle (pass level).
   b) Describe and justify your current lifestyle (merit level).
   c) Critically evaluate your current lifestyle (distinction level).

It would be a good idea to check that your answer is accurate and appropriate by showing it to your tutor at your next tutorial.

TOP TIP

When presenting evidence for an assessment, think about the person who will be looking through it. Plan your 'pitch' well and make it easy for the assessor to match your evidence against the grading criteria.

Sample assignment

Note about assignments

All learners are different and will approach their assignments in different ways. The sample assignment that follows shows how one learner answered a brief to achieve pass, merit and distinction level criteria. The learner's work shows just one way in which these grading criteria can be evidenced. There are no standard or set answers. If you produce the required evidence for each task then you will achieve the grading criteria covered by the assignment.

Sample assignment front sheet

Ensure that all the boxes on the front sheet are completed, including your name. Sign the declaration to show the work is yours.

Remember that you may be penalised for handing in work late. Always meet deadlines or your final grade might be affected.

Ask your tutor to give feedback on any draft work before submitting a final version to ensure that you have answered the tasks correctly and in the format required to meet the assessment criteria.

Learner name		Assessor name	
Edward Jaye		Michael Hayes	
Date issued	**Completion date**		**Submitted on**
20 September 2010	19 November 2010		17 November 2010
Qualification		**Unit**	
BTEC Level 3 Extended Diploma in IT		Unit 1 Communication and Employability Skills for IT	

Assignment title	Effective Communication

In this assessment you will have opportunities to provide evidence against the following criteria.
Indicate the page numbers where the evidence can be found.

Criteria reference	To achieve the criteria the evidence must show that the student is able to:	Task no.	Evidence
P4	Demonstrate a range of effective interpersonal skills	1	observation
P6	Communicate technical information to a specified audience	2	pages 1–2
M2	Review draft documents to produce final versions	2	pages 1–2
D1	Evaluate interpersonal and written communications techniques	3	pages 3–7
P5	Use IT to aid communications	4	throughout

Learner declaration
I certify that the work submitted for this assignment is my own and research sources are fully acknowledged.

Learner signature: *Edward Jaye*   Date: *17 November 2010*

You must check that the evidence you submit meets the requirements of each of these grading criteria.

The evidence you provide must be your own work, not copied from anywhere else. Where you do quote books, articles, etc. you must include a reference to the original source.

You must provide specific evidence to cover each of the grading criteria in this assignment. You need to list the pages in your assignment where the evidence is located.

Sample assignment brief

The scenario is essential. It sets the assignment in a real, vocational context.

The title is important. Always structure your work so it fits under this assessment title. Don't stray into other topic areas.

Qualification	Unit 1 Communication and Employability Skills for IT
Unit title	BTEC Level 3 Extended Diploma in IT
Start date	20 September 2010
Deadline date	19 November 2010
Assessor	Michael Hayes

Assignment title	Effective communication

The purpose of this assignment is to:
Demonstrate your proficiency in and knowledge of methods of communication

Scenario
You have been seconded to the Human Resources Department of the company for which you work in the management's hope that you can bring some IT expertise to the recruiting and training area of the business.

After creating a personal development plan for your time in the department, it is now time for you to demonstrate your ability to communicate effectively and to evaluate the various techniques used.

A lot of the evidence for criteria in this assignment can be taken from work elsewhere in this and other units, or even from other areas of your educational and social life.
Your tutor will act as your Human Resource Department line manager for the purpose of this assignment.

Task 1
You will need to gather together evidence of how effectively you have communicated with others face to face; what we call 'interpersonal skills'. This will involve:
a) Discussing any topic you like in a small group of 4–6 people. This could be research for another part of this unit, for a different unit, or for anything else social or academic. If you cannot devise a topic of your own, your line manager has a number of suggested topics which you can use. Your contribution to the group meeting will be observed and recorded.
b) Interacting with peers in class, with your friends socially, or with work colleagues if you have a part-time job. An observation record will be provided as evidence.
c) Undertaking a formal presentation on a topic of your choice.

Suitable evidence for all these activities can be in the form of a video, or a detailed witness statement/observation sheet backed up by notes (Word documents) and slides (PowerPoint).

(Criterion P4, part P5)

Task 2
a) You will gather together evidence of where you have written technical information for a specified audience.

Any document you have produced which contains technical information and is for a pre-specified audience will be acceptable.

You may have technical documents from elsewhere in your studies such as a detailed User Guide or technical documentation from a programming unit. Providing your audience for these is defined then you can use these as evidence.

If you are short of ideas then your line manager will be able to provide suitable topics.

Pay particular attention to the use of grammar, spelling, structure and relevance of material.

(Criterion P6, part P5)

b) Review this document and another of your own documents by using a spellchecker and by proofreading. Amend them as necessary to produce a final version, showing a before and after print for each. (The second document can be anything that you have produced.)
c) Review documents as produced by two of your peers and produce a list of amendments which would lead to a finished product. Print out your lists. If possible submit a copy of the original documents or ask your tutor to sign a statement to confirm that you have reviewed them correctly.

(Criterion M2, part P5)

This task is about interpersonal skills and communicating effectively with others. The topic of the communication is not important.

This task is about communicating in writing, the topic is not important, but it must be technical information you are communicating. You must demonstrate that you have communicated effectively, for example, by using language that is suitable for the audience and making sure there are no spelling or grammatical errors.

For this task you must evaluate the communications techniques you have demonstrated in Tasks 1 and 2. This is for a distinction criterion so you need to consider all of the points listed in detail.

You need to provide evidence of having carried out these tasks, such as screen shots or print outs of the emails.

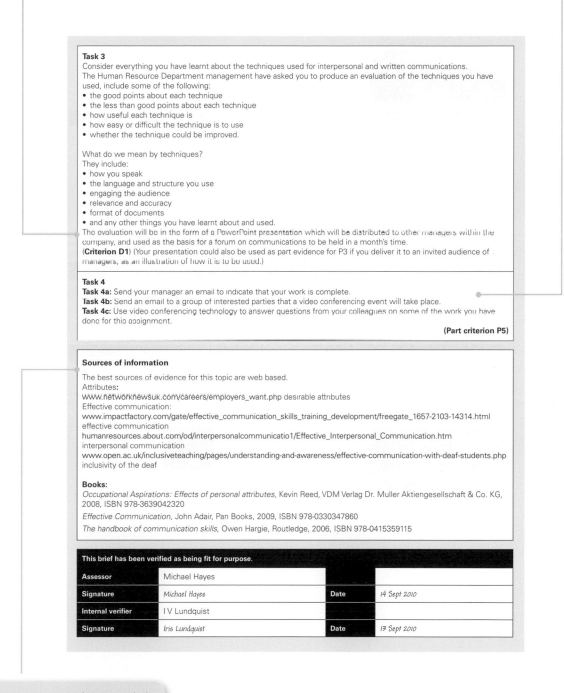

Task 3

Consider everything you have learnt about the techniques used for interpersonal and written communications.
The Human Resource Department management have asked you to produce an evaluation of the techniques you have used, include some of the following:
• the good points about each technique
• the less than good points about each technique
• how useful each technique is
• how easy or difficult the technique is to use
• whether the technique could be improved.

What do we mean by techniques?
They include:
• how you speak
• the language and structure you use
• engaging the audience
• relevance and accuracy
• format of documents
• and any other things you have learnt about and used.

The evaluation will be in the form of a PowerPoint presentation which will be distributed to other managers within the company, and used as the basis for a forum on communications to be held in a month's time.
(**Criterion D1**) (Your presentation could also be used as part evidence for P3 if you deliver it to an invited audience of managers, as an illustration of how it is to be used.)

Task 4

Task 4a: Send your manager an email to indicate that your work is complete.
Task 4b: Send an email to a group of interested parties that a video conferencing event will take place.
Task 4c: Use video conferencing technology to answer questions from your colleagues on some of the work you have done for this assignment.

(Part criterion P5)

Sources of information

The best sources of evidence for this topic are web based.
Attributes:
www.networknewsuk.com/careers/employers_want.php desirable attributes
Effective communication:
www.impactfactory.com/gate/effective_communication_skills_training_development/freegate_1657-2103-14314.html effective communication
humanresources.about.com/od/interpersonalcommunicatio1/Effective_Interpersonal_Communication.htm interpersonal communication
www.open.ac.uk/inclusiveteaching/pages/understanding-and-awareness/effective-communication-with-deaf-students.php inclusivity of the deaf

Books:
Occupational Aspirations: Effects of personal attributes, Kevin Reed, VDM Verlag Dr. Muller Aktiengesellschaft & Co. KG, 2008, ISBN 978-3639042320
Effective Communication, John Adair, Pan Books, 2009, ISBN 978-0330347860
The handbook of communication skills, Owen Hargie, Routledge, 2006, ISBN 978-0415359115

This brief has been verified as being fit for purpose.				
Assessor	Michael Hayes			
Signature	*Michael Hayes*	**Date**	*14 Sept 2010*	
Internal verifier	I V Lundquist			
Signature	*Iris Lundquist*	**Date**	*13 Sept 2010*	

These sources may be particularly useful for the evaluation you need to produce for Task 3.

Sample observation record for Task 1a (part P4)

This is a good example of the level of detail required in an observation record, completed by the teacher. This partially covers the evidence requirements for P4.

Learner name	Edward Jaye
Qualification	BTEC Level 3 Extended Diploma in IT
Unit number and title	Unit 1 Communication and Employability Skills for IT

Description of activity undertaken (please be as specific as possible)

Edward took part in a group activity to consider the attributes which are valued by employers. A group of four learners undertook research on different aspects of the topic then brought their research together to provide material from which they could individually present evidence for criterion P4.

Four meetings were held, one to allocate subject areas, two for progress reports and a final meeting to bring it all together.

Edward chaired the second meeting, showing skills in keeping to the point and leading and promoting the discussions that took place. He made significant contributions to all the other meetings, volunteering to take general attributes as his subject, and giving detailed progress reports before bringing his material to the final meeting.

He made several suggestions which helped the other members focus on their subject areas, and he was able to identify some of the problems they were having.

His contribution was always made sympathetically and he showed good interpersonal skills throughout.

Assessment and grading criteria

This work contributes to criterion P4 as a demonstration of one form of interpersonal skills.

A further two examples have been evidenced to provide for the full criterion to be awarded.

See observations relating to his peers and delivering a presentation.

This is evidence for P4 (part 1 of 3)

How the activity meets the requirements of the assessment and grading criteria

This activity was designed to provide evidence towards criterion P4 in that it shows interpersonal skills in a semi formal activity involving running and participating in small meetings.

The activity will be associated with interpersonal skills in an informal environment (i.e. with peer group) and in delivering a presentation – see separate evidence.

Learner signature	Edward Jaye	Date	15 October 2010
Assessor signature	Michael Hayes	Date	15 October 2010
Assessor name	Michael Hayes		

Sample observation record for Task 1b (part P4)

> This observation record partially covers the evidence requirements for P4.

Learner name	Edward Jaye
Qualification	BTEC Level 3 Extended Diploma in IT
Unit number and title	Unit 1 Communication and Employability Skills for IT

Description of activity undertaken (please be as specific as possible)

This is the second of the observed activities which contribute to the evidence for criterion P4. Edward's tutors have observed and recorded aspects of the way he relates to his peer group during normal class activity and in social times. He is good at expressing himself both verbally and with good use of body language, especially in responses where he will nod in encouragement and is good at listening. He can also be very determined if he wishes to make a point, and very forceful. Generally he is tolerant of other people's ideas, but good in verbal exchanges when he has a point to make. He has a certain amount of leadership potential when given a task within his group. Generally his interpersonal skills make him a well-liked and valued member of his peer group.

Assessment and grading criteria

This contributes to the range of interpersonal skills which have to be exhibited to gain the award of criterion P4.

A wide variety of skills were exhibited (see above) during observations of the more informal interactions with his peers.

This is evidence for P4 (part 2 of 3)

How the activity meets the requirements of the assessment and grading criteria

This activity was designed to provide evidence towards criterion P4 in that it shows interpersonal skills in a semi-formal activity involving running and participating in small meetings.

The activity will be associated with interpersonal skills in a more formal environment (i.e. meetings) and in delivering a presentation – see separate evidence.

Learner signature	Edward Jaye	Date	8 November 2010
Assessor signature	Michael Hayes	Date	8 November 2010
Assessor name	Michael Hayes		

The audience for this written piece of work is clearly stated.

The use of work from another unit to cover this criterion is good practice.

Sample learner work: page 1

Sample learner work for Task 2a P6

This is taken from evidence produced for Unit 13 (Human Computer Interaction) criterion D1:

Evaluate the HCI developments over recent years, relating them to the impact on society, economy and culture and predicting one potential future development and what impact it may have.

I have chosen to write an article for computer literate but non-technical adults.

The huge breadth of HCI development in recent years is testimony to the importance of this subject area to many areas of academic and business information programming. HCI as a subject seems these days to impact on everything from games design to applications and research in fields such as sociology and psychology. It is consequently quite difficult to select appropriate items for this article.

Similarly it is difficult to distinguish between impact on society, economy and culture since some developments impact on all three, but I have at least tried to relate developments to these areas. Accordingly I have selected some developments which I believe have had impacts in the three different areas.

Perhaps one of the most astounding pieces of human computer interaction in recent years in terms of culture, and possibly society, is the development of some of the modern games platforms. Most interestingly the Nintendo Wii and its myriad of accessories including steering wheels, balance boards and zappers (guns) as well as the more conventional control set. The Wii (pronounced 'we') is branded as a seventh generation games console which brought us a handheld wireless controller, the Wii remote, which acts as a handheld pointer and which detects movement in three dimensions. It gives the closest possible simulation, to actually playing sports and pastimes, of any games console so far.

The Wii allows you to play using the actual movements associated with the sports software you have purchased, and so realistic is this that there have been real attempts to market the system as a fitness machine. Software is available to simulate most sports, with tennis being particularly popular with my friends as is boxing and motor sport.

So good is the interface, and so interactive the virtual world graphics, that lessons learnt in their development have been incorporated in virtual reality training software for people who work in hazardous conditions.

The impact on 'culture' has been exceptional with families running group competitions, including inter-family competitions, as an alternative to other forms of entertainment, and other forms of fitness regimes.

The system has made some impact on the world economy, having now outsold its fiercest rivals (PlayStation 3 and Sony Xbox) and done so profitably by taking a different stance to the other two manufacturers. Microsoft and Sony both took the decision to loss lead with their system and gain on sales of software; Nintendo, it is rumoured, make profits on every sale of the hardware – not a direct economic impact perhaps, but a very interesting development.

Thinking of economic benefits, it is the sheer spread of different forms of HCI that has been the extraordinary development in this field. Easier input, faster input, automated input and input by people who have not been able to use systems before, have all contributed to economic benefits. New forms of input are the basis of much of this with text readers, voice recognition and even research into 'thought' recognition. All of these developments allow for a greater throughput of transactions by the same number or less people than previous systems – they make a great contribution to organisations which employ them.

Developments also include output in forms devised to make it easier use for many different groups of people. Tactile and speech output for the visually challenged mean that these people can now undertake jobs which were not available to them before. Speech output has also made major improvements to systems such as timetable information.

A major contribution has also been made by anomaly display, where only the results that are not consistent with normal operation are actually displayed. This has meant that scanning results for problems is a lot less onerous and can be done by a smaller number of people.

This work is sufficiently technical in its content but avoids the use of complex technical explanations and jargon. It clearly focuses on applications of HCI, which suits the stated audience.

Sample learner work: page 2

In terms of society and probably economy, one of the most revolutionary HCI developments of the last decade or so has been the increased development of things like the fly by wire system for aircraft. Essentially in this system, which first came from military jets, the pilot instructs the on-board computers what they want to do – turn to port, climb, roll, etc, normally with a joystick type control, and the computer then manoeuvres the controls to make the aircraft perform accordingly.

It was really the transition for use in civil aircraft which made this a major player in HCI. We now have civil aircraft which could not exist without the system; the Airbus 320 for instance could not be landed by two pilots using manual controls – they just could not react quickly enough to the adjustments of attitude and speed required to land this aircraft. The fly by wire system allows the aircraft to be flown by the same number of crew as the previous generation of aircraft. It also means that we can build aircraft which are lighter, more fuel efficient, easier to build and so on which could not have existed before; a great economic benefit as well.

As an extension of this, the military use head-up displays and line of sight controls. Basically pilots only have to look in a particular direction for the plane to turn in that direction, and other controls are also coupled into the head set. Head-up displays can work in several ways, but all of them essentially display information in view without a person having to move their head to look down at controls.

I think that it is in this area that there is potential for future developments. Why not drive by wire and head-up displays for drivers, particularly for trucks or perhaps cranes. In some ways this could lead to a de-skilling of some jobs and consequent economic benefit. It could also bring about consistent accuracy in the use of the machinery and help to counter human error which is the cause of so many accidents. This is, in my opinion, a possibility for developments in the future.

Sample learner work for Task 2b M2

Proofreading own material
[The learner supplied two lengthy pieces of work that he had produced during his course. The first was speaker notes to accompany a PowerPoint presentation on the theme of communication (reproduced later in this publication). The second was a text en titled HCI Evaluation (reproduced earlier in this publication). Both pieces of work had 'before' and 'after' versions. The 'before' version showed the original, unproofread material, which included numerous spelling mistakes, layout errors and typing mistakes. The 'after' version showed where these mistakes had been picked up by the learner during the proofreading process. The learner also included a summary of the changes made to both pieces of work.]

Criterion P6 is covered by this piece of work.

In a 'real' assignment these before and after versions should be submitted.

Sample observation record for Task 2b (part P5)

This observation record, along with the before and after versions of the work, provides evidence for M2 and also contributes towards P5.

Learner name	Edward Jaye
Qualification	BTEC Level 3 Extended Diploma in IT
Unit number and title	Unit 1 Communication and Employability Skills for IT

Description of activity undertaken (please be as specific as possible)

Edward has proofread two written reports, one by Sylvia Machem entitled 'Purpose and features of operating systems' and one by Abdul Mansari entitled 'Working in e-commerce'. I have seen him make corrections to spelling, grammar and construction which resulted in the document, once updated, being in a suitable form for final presentation.

Assessment and grading criteria

This work contributes to assessment criterion M2 in that it provides evidence of Edward proofreading others' draft documents and producing a final version after corrections have been made.

Edward has also used spellchecking software which contributes to the evidence for criterion P5.

How the activity meets the requirements of the assessment and grading criteria

The proofreading of the learner's own materials – which I have also observed and for which there are before and after printouts – and the proofreading and correcting of others' work provides full evidence for criterion M2.

Learner signature	Edward Jaye	Date	8 November 2010
Assessor signature	Michael Hayes	Date	8 November 2010
Assessor name	Michael Hayes		

For a distinction criterion there is too much detail to include in the PowerPoint slides alone, so the speakers notes have also been included.

Sample learner work: page 3

Sample learner work for Task 3 (D1)

(Also used in evidence for Task 1c P4, and part P5)

Slide 1:

Evaluation of Communication Techniques
Interpersonal skills
Written communications

This presentation will look at some of the techniques which are used for communication and will evaluate how useful and successful they are.

Interpersonal skills refer to the skills needed to communicate with people in person, face to face.

This might be on a one to one basis, one to many as in a presentation and many to many as in meetings.

Written communications refer to any form such as letters, articles and emails.

Slide 2:

Interpersonal skills
• Delivery method
• Cues
• Language
• Engagement

We will be reviewing and evaluating these headings and some of the techniques within them.

Delivery method for interpersonal skills is normally the voice, but doesn't need to be and we will look at the advantages and disadvantages of a few methods.

Cues cover things like body language, intonation and gestures.

When we talk about language we will look at positive and negative language, structure and vocabulary.

Engagement refers to ways in which we can get people to run along with us, keep attention and participate where necessary.

We can also add barriers to this list, or techniques we can use to reduce the affect of barriers. Explaining these techniques has been done elsewhere in the unit, but here we might mention a couple of points and talk about their effectiveness.

Slide 3:

Delivery method
• Verbal
• Signing
• Lip reading

The normal method of interpersonal communication is by the human voice. In the majority of cases this is an ideal method since people recognise voices, understand the voice intonation and feel comfortable with an experienced speaker. It is a method we are

all used to and there is something comforting in hearing someone speaking to us and in responding in the same way. Voices can be very expressive and can be used to stress the importance of things which the written page does not. But to be really successful the person must be an accomplished speaker and must be able to deliver what they say in a clear and interesting manner. Against is the fact that not everyone is an accomplished speaker – some voices jar on our nerves, some are bland and uninteresting – it depends more on the characteristics of the person than does the written page. There are also places where straightforward talking is not appropriate. Very quiet places or very noisy places for instance, and also where people cannot hear very well.

For those who are aurally challenged a system of signing has been developed, in fact there are at least two different systems. Skilful use of signing, coupled with body language about which we will hear later, can relay the same sense of purpose and importance as purely vocal communication. Signing is excellent for those who cannot hear, but it does need learning and unless we have an audience which regularly relies on it then it is something with which the public in general do not relate.

Lip reading is another form of delivery which most of us do sub-consciously. As I said, it is something we use especially when we want to communicate in places which are very quiet or very noisy. The cotton mills of Lancashire were extremely noisy places and all of the operatives learned to communicate by lip reading – it is often said that the Lancashire accent owes more to the forming of words for people to lip read than to actually speaking. Lip reading does, to a large extent, rely on the deliverer forming words properly with their lips; it is much more of a skill than merely speaking without having to make a sound. Learning to lip read relies heavily on the reader understanding the accent or dialect of the speaker. It is a useful addition for people who do not hear too well but as a regular method of communication it lacks the flexibility of the voice or indeed of signing.

Slide 4:

Cues
• Facial expression
• Body language
• Intonation

The title 'Cues' might be misleading, but I can't think of a different one. What I am going to talk about is the use of non-verbal actions to emphasise, or add to, verbal communication.

This demonstrates good coverage of the methods of communication as listed in the Unit Content.

Detailed evaluation has been provided of the advantages and disadvantages of different techniques.

Sample learner work: page 4

In Britain by far the most important of these 'cues' is facial expression. We are used to people pulling faces, in the widest sense, as they talk. Therefore we can detect sorrow, joy, disgust, pity and so on just by looking at a face. This is useful when speaking to people; they can pick up the mood of what is being said by your facial expression. It is probably at its most useful amongst friends and informally, although its skilful use can play a major role in presentations where a particular mood has to be set. The danger is that we get so used to using facial expressions to convey points that we may use them without thinking – talking enthusiastically about something in which we do not believe, whilst our face might tell the real story!

In some cultures it is the eyes which tell the full story, and our eyes rarely lie even when the rest of our face is conforming to what we are saying. There is little we can do about this except try to deflect attention from our eyes by gestures, slides, etc.

Body language is about gestures and posture, and this has a high priority in some cultures. In Italy for instance, body language is almost a separate means of communication in that the same spoken words using different gestures can mean totally different things. Body language is vital to all our interpersonal communication. Relaxed posture adds to the confidence of an audience at a presentation. In small meetings and informal groups body language can convey all emotions from anger to joy and everything in between. Hand gestures play a major role, the pointing, the making of a fist, broad sweeps of the arms and so on can all be used to emphasise points we wish to make. We can utilise a knowledge of body language to emphasise points or to give out a certain impression of who we are and what we portray; use them to our advantage. A famous actor of the last century when about to make an exit from the stage, always used to take a step forward before he moved in the direction of his exit; it emphasised his role. As with facial expression, we have to be careful that, by accident, we do not contradict by body language that which we are saying. Another negative point is that too many gestures can act as a distraction and mean that people watch the gestures rather than take in what is being conveyed.

Intonation, or voice modulation as it is sometimes known, is another method of emphasising a point. Stressing particular words by changing the way we deliver them so that they stand out from our regular tone of voice. We can use both loudness and softness to emphasise points we need to make. The normal thing to do if we want to stress a point is to shout louder, but it is not always the most helpful. Several very successful politicians have, for instance, learned to speak more softly to emphasise a point, sometimes to move back from a microphone and speak more softly so that people have to really listen. Sometimes different intonation can be used to convey sarcasm or irony and emphasise a point in that way. We need to be able to learn such techniques, and view their effect on other people; this is not always as easy as we would believe.

These techniques in general need to be practised to provide the effect that we most desire to convey.

```
Language
• Positive
• Negative
```

Slide 5:

There are aspects involved with both interpersonal and written communications.

Here, I just want to mention two aspects of language, positive and negative.

In both cases we need to look at verbs, vocabulary, structure and delivery.

The differentiation here is quite slight, differences which are called nuances.

For instance consider the following two responses to a query:
"We will not be able to get it done until Friday"
"We will definitely get it done on Friday"

Essentially they mean the same thing – but which is positive and which is negative in the impression of the person being addressed?

We have to think carefully about how we structure our words and phrases; a slight change of verb or tense can easily change the meaning of a phrase from positive and encouraging to negative. This is another thing which takes practice to use to our advantage – we can even use it deliberately to put a less than enthusiastic slant onto something which we are promoting and vice versa.

The down side is that we can unfortunately quite innocently change the tone if we do not carefully prepare in advance.

A useful technique therefore is to carefully read through what you are going to say, attempting to ensure that the tone is positive throughout unless, of course you want to give a negative impression.

> Correctly, the accompanying slides only display bulleted summery text. It is the speaker's notes which add the detail.

Sample learner work: page 5

Slide 6:

There are lots of different ways in which you can engage with an audience and we have only time to mention one or two here.

Engagement is about keeping the attention of the audience, and about them being involved in some way. Attractive slides, discussions, humour, all help. Allowing limited questions during the delivery and asking the audience questions as you go along are both ways of engaging with them. Summarising and paraphrasing at regular intervals is also a help, especially when coupled with questions you will ask them. Once again this takes practice, ensuring that audience involvement and participation do not interfere with the flow of what you are trying to do e.g. questions are best dealt with a special breakpoints and should be restricted time wise.

When you are yourself listening to someone talking you should try to find out what actually bores you, because it will also bore other people. It is also good to respond occasionally with a sympathetic nod of the head, or a suitable question.

These are all easy things to say but difficult techniques to learn, and it is easy to get them wrong. For instance:

- allowing questions during delivery can descend into a verbal fracas if you are not careful.
- when listening, too frequent nods of the head are just as off putting as none at all
- too many funny stories might mean that all that is remembered is the funny story, not the message
- decorative slides can become overpowering
- allowing open questions rather than closed questions can be a distraction; it is far better to accept questions on a ring fenced area of the presentation than to allow open questions.

Beware is the watchword, the balance is difficult to obtain and needs practice.

Barriers have been dealt with elsewhere and are only included here for completeness. Many of the techniques which can be used to counteract barriers depend on good initial preparation. Environment, distractions and audience type are the main barriers.

Slide 7:

A brief look at four of the basics of communication in writing, although to what extent these can be declare techniques is debatable. There are many more items which could be included, but here I have concentrated on what I think of as the basics and the techniques which surround them.

Slide 8:

Whilst grammar and spelling are in themselves not 'techniques' they attract many techniques to get them right, and we all need to be aware of these.

In many ways the spelling and grammar cause impressions, good and bad, which are well above their 'punching weight'.

By that I mean that the sense of what you are trying to write can often be delivered irrespective of whether the grammar and spelling is correct, but it is one of the first things people notice.

Once spotted, poor grammar and poor spelling create a bad impression, and very often weigh on peoples' minds. Sometimes the jar the nerves of a reader so badly that they become a total distraction and the whole point of a document can be lost.

Software comes to our aid since we have spelling checks, grammar checks and even a thesaurus available to help, but beware since all is not what it seems.

Spelling checks only check to see if the word exists – they do not check the sense of the thing hence 'to', 'too' and 'two' are all valid words but have different use. They are useful in doing a first sift of the text to rule out all non-existent words and downright bad spelling. It is a technique to which we should all subscribe.

Grammar checks are not over helpful in that they seem to follow strange rules at times, demanding changes to phrases which are perfectly sensible. Most people find these less than helpful and the majority do not use them; optional use which might be helpful at times.

These PowerPoint slides could be enhanced with the use of colours, backgrounds and some relevant images. Including a video clip, perhaps of different types of body language, would enhance them further.

Sample learner work: page 6

So we should use a spellchecker, very easy to use and understand, and very worthwhile despite its limitations.

How then do we check grammar and spellchecker errors? Proofreading. We need to studiously read the text through until we have identified as many errors as possible, and then, if it is a published text, have someone else check it for errors as well. We don't need special skills to do this, just time and patience – there are special symbols used by proof checkers to indicate errors, but we don't have to use them to be able to do this.

Proofreading is difficult; it takes time; it needs concentration. It is however, a technique which we should definitely use where our written work is to be publicly viewed, and a skill we should all try to gain.

Using someone else to proofread your work is also important since you may well miss errors you have made yourself, but a new pair of eyes approaches it from a different perspective.

Slide 9:

Structure
- Single block
- Columns
- Tabular
- Use of illustrations
- Use of colour and font

The simplest form of structure for written communications is as a single block of text.

This is quite useful where some important information has to be imparted to people who are awaiting that information and it is fine to use this style for novels, because that is what people expect, or for a letter or memo.

It would be wrong for a newspaper these days, or for a user manual, because our expectations are different for those documents.

The style in which it is written can lend to the impact by using humour, dialogue, illustrations, etc.

Other techniques which are involved are the justification left, centre, right and fully justified which need to be used with care, the default being left justified. This may leave a very ragged right had edge with a ragged left had edge from right justified and two ragged edges with centred. This may suggest that fully justified has a fairly universal appeal, but it needs care since the justification is done by inserting extra spaces into the line of text, and sometimes this is not done totally sympathetically.

We can use this structure where it is expected but it has limitations for certain uses, we need to take care that we use it appropriately, and use our writing and illustrating techniques to make it more acceptable.

Writing in columns is a useful technique where a newspaper or journal type article is being produced. It is the standard format for such writing and is expected, but is less useful for things like letters, memos and minutes. It is a technique with limitations which we need to learn, and to use it appropriately. Less useful than the 'single block' style in terms of the number of applications to which it is applicable but a worthy technique to learn especially where we will be involved in the preparation of newspaper and journal articles. It is a relatively easy technique to use since most of the formatting work is done automatically by the software.

Tabular communications are useful for things like columns of figures in numerical reports, formatting documents like sales invoices, drawing up minutes of meeting and tables of comparison. A limited variety of uses but a useful technique where it has a purpose. Once again it needs care in use since it is easy to spoil the look of a document by the injudicious use of tables. More limited use than single block and columns.

Illustrations, as we have already said, can be used to make the material more approachable. Besides adding clarity to the narrative – it is often said that a picture is worth 1000 words – they also break up the text and the effort of concentration required to read mass text. As we shall mention on the next slide they must be relevant – have some meaning within the subject of the text, or add something significant to the meaning of the text. Never, ever should an illustration be added just to add variety. Placement of illustrations is another technique which needs to be acquired; to the left with text flowing round to the right; to the right with text flowing round to the left; centrally with text flowing right round; or with text terminating above and recommencing below. Care must be taken in not using too many illustrations in a text because then they lose their impact. All of this needs skill; the use of illustrations sounds quite easy but to use them correctly is quite difficult. The benefit is that used properly they bring a text to life.

Use of colour and different fonts and sizes can also be used for emphasis, but once again it is a matter of a few inclusions to make the most impact. Again skill and judgement are what is required. Too much colour and too many fonts and sizes not only lose impact, but look messy and may cause potential readers to dismiss the text before they have read it.

Source references should be included. They should list the books (author, title, publisher, date of publication and ISBN number) and web sites used in this assignement.

Sample learner work: page 7

Slide 10:

Relevance

· Relating to the subject
· No spurious inclusions
· Inclusions used for effect

Generally everything within the written communication should relate to its subject.

Illustrations and anecdotes should add to the text and not be totally spurious.

Everything must be relevant, a totally spurious inclusion is a distraction which should not be used.

Skill is required to determine what is relevant and to what degree it is relevant.

Slide 11:

Language

· Appropriate
· Precision

Language must be appropriate to the type of communication.

Journalistic for newsletters, plain English for non-specialists, technical for specialists, informal for friends, etc.

Writers must be able to identify the language and style requirement.

Using the wrong linguistic style will put off targeted readers and your message will be lost.

For the same reason the language you use must also be precise in description and explanation.

These are skills which come only with practice, but are vital to acquire if written communication is to be effective.

Difficult to develop but worth doing so.

That completes our brief summary of the techniques used for communication.

Are there any further questions?

This presentation covers D1 and provide evidence towards P5.

Sample observation record for Task 3 (D1, P4 and P5)

This is the observation record for the learner giving the presentation they produced for D1. By actually giving the presentation, evidence is provided towards P4 and P5.

Learner name	Edward Jaye
Qualification	BTEC Level 3 Extended Diploma in IT
Unit number and title	Unit 1 Communication and Employability Skills for IT

Description of activity undertaken (please be as specific as possible)

PowerPoint presentation to evaluate the techniques used for interpersonal skills and written communications

Assessment and grading criteria

The presentation is used to provide evidence for the evaluation in criterion D1. This observation together with the PowerPoint slides and speaker's notes provide full evidence for criterion D1.

The delivery of the presentation is also used as evidence towards P4 and P5.

How the activity meets the requirements of the assessment and grading criteria

Edward delivered the material competently, with confidence and understanding. The audience comprised tutors and peers role-playing the management of the company for which he worked. Where the audience were unclear or felt that the material was incomplete they were allowed to ask questions and these were fielded with knowledge and professionalism.

Defining what are the 'techniques' used is quite tricky since they are not defined as such in the unit specifications. We have therefore left the learners to try to identify 'techniques' themselves from the material we have supplied and from the unit specifications. This has been done quite expertly by Edward as can be seen from the speaker's notes and slides. My observation can attest to the additional information, especially as a result of questions asked. In places some of the elements described are not what might realistically be called techniques, but always Edward has associated them with important techniques. There was also some question about the overall evaluative nature of the presentation yet Edward pointed out benefits and adverse effects, he spoke of where items can be used effectively and where they may cause problems and as such there is no doubt that this material is evaluative.

Learner signature	Edward Jaye	Date	27 October 2010
Assessor signature	Michael Hayes	Date	27 October 2010
Assessor name	Michael Hayes		

These two emails provide evidence towards P5. To further enhance the authenticity of the evidence, these emails could have included the email header (to, from, subject, etc.).

Sample learner work for Task 4a (part P5)

Dear Harry

My training on developing my communication skills is now at an end and I have completed all of the work requested.

I will naturally be hoping to continue developing these skills as I progress, but this initial phase is now complete, and I can hopefully move on to my next project in the department.

This work has been interesting and I believe I have learnt many useful things.

Regards

Edward

Sample learner work for Task 4b (part P5)

Hi everyone

There will be a video conferencing event on Friday 23 April commencing at 12:00 where you will be able to question me on all aspects of effective comunication.

A leaflet is attached with further details.

Please try to attend.

Regards

Edward

Sample observation record for Task 4c (part P5)

This shows the observation record detailing the use of video conferencing. Additional evidence could include a short video clip or a photograph of the learner using the system. This provides evidence towards P5.

Learner name	Edward Jaye
Qualification	BTEC Level 3 Extended Diploma in IT
Unit number and title	Unit 1 Communication and Employability Skills for IT

Description of activity undertaken (please be as specific as possible)

Edward used the video conferencing system to speak to people in other parts of our building and to answer questions on effective communication. He did this competently, managing to get connected and to use the equipment without any help from his tutors.

He also used the email system competently, both sending and receiving emails to single and groups of people. During the work for this unit he has competently used word processing, presentation software and proofing software in addition to email and video conferencing.

Assessment and grading criteria

The observation record provides evidence for criterion P5 when taken together with the other documentary evidence in this unit.

How the activity meets the requirements of the assessment and grading criteria

The observation and documentary material cover WP, PowerPoint, proofing, other (email) and web-based (VC) which are the elements of IT specifically stated as prescriptive in the unit content.

Learner signature	Edward Jaye	Date	15 October 2010
Assessor signature	Michael Hayes	Date	15 October 2010
Assessor name	Michael Hayes		

Sample assessor's comments

When completing the assignment it is useful for you to add your own feedback on what you felt went well and what didn't. This may help with future assignments and may also help the tutor to produce a better version of the assignment next year.

You need to make sure you complete at least all the pass criteria, otherwise you will fail the unit.

Qualification	BTEC Level 3 Extended Diploma in IT	Assessor name	M Hayes
Unit number and title	Unit 1 Communication and Employability Skills for IT	Learner name	E Jaye

Grading criteria	Achieved?
P4 Demonstrate a range of effective interpersonal skills	Y
P6 Communicate technical information to a specified audience	Y
M2 Review draft documents to produce final versions	Y
D1 Evaluate interpersonal and written communication techniques	Y
P5 Use IT to aid communications a) Word processing b) Presentation c) Email d) Video conference e) Proofing	Y Task 2 Task 3 Task 4 Task 4 Task 2

Learner feedback

A difficult assignment, even for a more mature type of student like me. I found it difficult to provide evidence of things which I do naturally.

Assessor feedback

This is a well put together piece of work which is worthy of the award of all targeted criteria.
Criterion **P4** is evidenced mainly by my observation and by some video evidence which is stored here at the centre. This is acceptable.

There is a nice, perhaps short, technical paper based around HCI for criterion **P6**; well done; it definitely puts ideas forward to a non-technical audience.

Evidence for **M2** is a mixture of before and after prints of own reports together with some notes and observations. A good piece of work demonstrating you are highly proficient in this area.

The evaluation for **D1** by using a slide display is always novel but you have done this well. At first glance I did wonder if it was evaluative, but in seeing you deliver this it became clear that you had made evaluative judgements at almost every stage.

Evidence for criterion **P5** has been shown in several aspects of the work and accumulated to cover the whole of the criterion.

Well done for some excellent work.

Action plan

N/A

Assessor signature	Michael Hayes	Date	22 November 2010
Learner signature	Edward Jaye	Date	26 November 2010

Read the assessor feedback carefully as it will help you identify what you did well and what you need to do to improve.

The action plan is particularly important as it tells you what you need to do to achieve any grades you have not passed.

Make notes on how you would do this assignment.

Step Seven: Work productively as a member of a group

Case study: The difficulties of teamwork

For her second assignment for Unit 4: Impact of the Use of IT on Business Systems Alice needed to work as a member of a group. This wasn't something she was particularly keen on, especially as the teacher had chosen the groups and she wasn't working with any of her friends. There were three others in her group; they were okay, but she would have preferred to be with her friends.

The group didn't get off to a very good start as they argued about who should do what. Someone suggested that they appoint a team leader. They all agreed this would be a good idea but it took a long time to decide who this should be and, in the end, one member of the team, Steve, was not at all happy with the choice of leader as he thought it should have been him. All of the discussions and arguments had been time-consuming and there wasn't much time left to carry out the tasks they had to do. Steve went off and worked on his own to do one of the tasks. Alice worked on another task with Anita, while the remaining task was left to Mohammed, the fourth team member. They didn't meet up as a whole team again, and when it came to handing in the work they discovered that Steve had duplicated a lot of the work that Alice and Anita had done, while Mohammed had not completed his task.

Reflection points

Why is working in a group often more difficult than working on your own?

What steps do you think Alice's team could have taken in order to work together more successfully?

In your private life, you can choose your own friends, whereas at work you are paid to work alongside many people; whether you like them or not.

This applies at school or college too. Hopefully, by now, you've outgrown wanting to only work with your best friends on every project.

You may not be keen on everyone in your team, but you should still be pleasant and co-operative. This may be harder if you are working with a partner than in a large group.

Sometimes you may be the group leader. This may inspire you, or fill you with dread. You won't be expected to develop team-leader skills overnight, but it helps if you know the basics.

First, you should understand how groups and teams work and why good teamwork is considered vital by employers.

Working in groups and teams

If you have a full- or part-time job, you already belong to a working group, or team. At school or college your class is an example of a working group.

All working groups have some common characteristics:

- doing the same type of work – though in the workplace you probably have different roles or responsibilities
- a group leader or supervisor
- a reason for working together, such as studying for the same qualification or tackling an area of work too large for someone to do alone
- group members are dependent on each other in some way; at work you may have to cover someone's workload if they are absent
- group members concentrate on their individual achievements and success.

A team is different. As a team member you have a specific objective to achieve **together** – and this is more important than the goals of individual team members.

TOP TIP

Understanding how groups and teams function will help you be a better team worker and a better team leader.

These are the characteristics of a team.

- Team members have a team goal which is more important than any personal goals.
- Team members have complementary skills so that the team can achieve more than individuals working alone could achieve.
- Work is allocated to play to each person's strengths and talents.
- The team members give each other encouragement and support.
- There is collective responsibility for achieving the goal.

A good team leader acts as facilitator and motivator, and gives practical support and guidance.

Working in a team has many benefits. Team members can learn from each other and combine their skills to do a better job more quickly. Working with other people is often more enjoyable than working alone, too. Many industries rely heavily on efficient group working, from IT teams to health workers and the emergency services.

TOP TIP

Focusing on the task rather than on personalities is the first step in learning to work with different people, whose views may not match your own.

There are many benefits to be gained from working as a team.

Being a good team member

Everyone wants team members who are talented, positive, cheerful and full of energy. These are the key areas to focus on if you wish to be a good team member.

- **Your social skills.** This includes being courteous, treating other people as you wish to be treated, saying 'please' when you want something and thanking people who do you a favour.

- **Your temperament**. Expect people to have different views and opinions from you and don't take offence if someone disagrees with you. If you lose your temper easily, learn to walk away before you say something you may regret.

- **Your communication skills.** This includes talking and listening!

Practise saying what you mean clearly, accurately and succinctly. Be prepared to give good reasons to justify your arguments and ideas.

Allow people to finish what they're saying, without interruption, before you talk. Never shout people down. Think before you speak so that you don't upset people with tactless remarks. If you inadvertently do so, apologise.

- **Your commitment.** Always keep your promises and never let anyone down when they are depending upon you. Always do your fair share of the work, even if you don't agree with all the decisions made by your team. Tell people promptly if you are having problems so there is time to solve them. Be loyal to your team when you're talking to other people.

Being the team leader

It can be difficult to strike a balance between 'leading' the team and working with friends. You need to inspire and motivate your team without being bossy or critical.

Important points to remember about being a team leader

- Lead by example. Stay pleasant, consistent and control your temper, even under pressure.

- Everyone is different. Your ways of working may not always be the best.

- Be prepared to listen and contribute positively to a discussion.

- Encourage quieter team members to join in discussions by asking for their views.

- Be prepared to do whatever you ask other people to do.

- Note down what you say you will do, so that you don't forget.

- Discuss alternatives with people rather than giving orders.

- Be sensitive to other people's feelings. They may have personal problems or issues that affect their behaviour.

- Learn the art of persuasion.

- Act as peacemaker. Help people reach a compromise when necessary.

- Give team members the credit for their hard work or good ideas.

- Admit your mistakes. Look for a positive solution and think about what can be learned for the future, rather than making excuses.

- Praise and encourage team members who are working hard.

- Make criticisms constructively, and in private.

- Be assertive (put forward your point of view firmly) rather than aggressive (attacking other people to defend yourself.)

Some notes of caution about being a team leader

- Try to look pleasant and don't glare at people who interrupt you unexpectedly.

- Never talk about team members behind their backs.

- Don't gossip, exaggerate to make a point, spread rumours, speculate or tell lies.

- Don't expect to get your own way all the time – all good leaders back down on occasion.

- Never criticise any colleagues in front of other people. Speak to them in private and keep it constructive.

TOP TIP

Excellent ideas often come from quiet team members. Encourage everyone to make suggestions so that you don't overlook any valuable contributions.

Key points

- There are many benefits of working in a group or as a team. These include mutual support, companionship and the exchange of ideas.

- You will be expected to work co-operatively with other people at work, and during many course assignments.

- It isn't easy learning to be a team leader. Team leaders should be fair, consistent and pleasant to work with, as well as loyal and sensitive to the needs of team members.

Action points

1 Identify the role of teamwork in your area of study. Identify the team's goal and any factors you think will contribute towards its success.

2 Decide how you would handle each of the following difficult situations if you were the team leader. If you can, discuss your ideas with a friend in your class.

a) The team needs to borrow a college video camera to record an event being held tonight. Your tutor tells you that the one you reserved last week is not working and the rest are out on loan.

b) A member of your team has personal problems so you have given him less work to do. Now you've been accused of having favourites.

c) A team member is constantly letting everyone down because of poor work and non-attendance at group meetings.

d) Two team members have disagreed about how to do a task. You're not bothered how they do it as long as it gets done properly, and by the deadline.

e) A team member becomes very aggressive whenever she is challenged in any way – no matter how mildly.

3 Identify someone who has inspired you because they've been an excellent leader. This could be someone you've met, a fictional character or a famous person. Note down what it is about them that impressed you.

The captain leads and motivates the team to succeed.

Activity: Working in a group

Working in a group can be difficult but it is an important skill to develop and something employers are keen for you to have. Work in IT is often carried out in teams. For example, if you are developing a new computer game, you will work as part of a project team that might include junior and senior programmers, designers, graphics specialists and artists, people who work on the music and so on. Some members of the team might even work in different countries.

Think of strategies you could use to deal with the following group-work problems.

Problem	How could you deal with it?
The group cannot decide who to appoint as a team leader	
The team leader is too bossy and won't listen to what anyone says	
One person in the group keeps making rude remarks about other people in the group	
The group cannot decide how to divide up the tasks between the group members	
One member of the group is not doing the tasks they have been allocated	

Working well in a group means you need to behave in a certain way and stick to certain rules. Can you think of four or five rules or guidelines for effective group working?

1	
2	
3	
4	
5	

TOP TIP

Remember – you are part of a team as well as an individual so you will need to establish a balance between the two.

Step Eight: Understand how to research and analyse information

Case study: Researching and organising information

For Unit 7: Organisational Systems Security, Simon has to write a guide on the IT security threats that face an organisation. Some of his friends on the course have told him to copy information on viruses from the internet, but he knows that this is not the correct way to research information. He also knows that copying and pasting information from the internet and claiming it as your own is plagiarism – this is not allowed on any BTEC course and could mean your assignment is rejected and has to be done again.

Fortunately, Simon listens to his tutor's advice: 'Our tutor told us that security is a rapidly changing area and that we need to keep up to date with the latest developments by reading magazines and newspapers, and checking internet resources like news websites for information. I have been doing this and keeping a scrapbook of articles since the start of the unit.'

Simon's scrapbook proves very useful for this assignment. In addition, his tutor also arranges for an IT manager from a local company to come in and talk to the students about the security issues the company faces. Simon takes careful notes during the talk and is able to use this information in his assignment.

To get his information organised, Simon uses headings about the main security threats by looking at his lesson notes and the Unit Content in the specification. He then finds an example for each heading from either the notes he wrote during the IT manager's talk or from his scrapbook.

'For each example from a magazine or website, I wrote an introductory paragraph explaining the issue in my own words. Then I quoted a paragraph from the article which summaries or explains it well. I also listed the source of the quote. Our tutor explained that by making it clear that the quote is not my work and it comes from another source, this is not plagiarism and is a legitimate way of explaining something in an assignment.'

Reflection points

Think about how you research information. Are your current techniques effective?

How do you think you could use information you have gathered, talks you have heard or visits you have been on in your assignments?

As a BTEC Level 3 National learner, you often have to find information for yourself. This skill will be invaluable in your working life, and if you continue your studies at higher education (HE) level. Sometimes the information will give you a better understanding of a topic, at other times you will research to obtain information for a project or assignment. Sometimes you may be so interested in something that you want to find out more without being told to do so!

Whatever your reason, and no matter where your information can be found, there is a good and not so good way to go about the task. This section will help if you can't find what you want, or find too much, or drift aimlessly around a library, or watch a demonstration and don't know what to ask afterwards.

Types of information

There are many types of information and many different sources. Depending on the task, these are the sources you may need to consult.

- **Verbal information.** This includes talking to friends, colleagues at work, members of your family, listening to experts explain what they do, interviewing people, talking to sales reps at an exhibition or customers about a product.

- **Printed information**. This includes information printed in newspapers, journals, magazines, books, posters, workshop manuals, leaflets and catalogues. The type of magazine or newspaper you read may have its own slant on the information, which you may have to take into account (see page 73).

- **Written information**. This includes course notes and handouts, reports and other documents in the workplace. If you want to use written information from work, you must check this is allowed, and that it doesn't contain confidential material such as financial information or staff names and addresses.

- **Graphical information.** This includes illustrations, pictures, cartoons, line drawings, graphs and photographs. Graphics can make something clearer than words alone. For example, a satnav instruction book might contain illustrations to show different procedures.

- **Electronic information.** This includes information from electronic sources such as DVDs, CD-ROMs, searchable databases, websites, podcasts, webinars (**seminars** online), emails and text messages. The huge amount of information available online is both a help and a hindrance. You can find information quickly, but the source may be unreliable, out-of-date, inaccurate or inappropriate (see pages 66–67).

TOP TIP

Too much information is as bad as too little, because it's overwhelming. The trick is to find good quality, relevant information and know when to call a halt to your search.

TOP TIP

Consider all appropriate sources and don't just rely on information found online.

Finding what you need

Spend a few minutes planning what to do before you start looking for information. This can save a lot of time later on.

The following steps will help you to do this.

1 Make sure you understand exactly what it is you need to know so that you don't waste time looking for the wrong thing.

2 Clarify your objectives to narrow down your search. Think about why the information is wanted and how much detail you need. For example, learners studying BTEC Nationals in Engineering and Performing Arts may both be researching 'noise' for their projects but they are likely to need different types of information and use it in different ways.

3 Identify your sources and check you know how to use them. You need to choose sources that are most likely to provide information relevant to your objectives. For example, an Engineering learner might find information on noise emissions in industry journals and by checking out specialist websites.

4 Plan and schedule your research. Theoretically, you could research information forever. Knowing when to call a halt takes skill. Write a schedule that states when you must stop looking and start sorting the information.

5 Store your information safely in a labelled folder. This folder should include printouts or photocopies of articles, notes about events you have attended or observed, photographs you've taken or sketches you've drawn. Divide your information under topic headings to make it easier to find. When you're ready to start work, re-read your assignment brief and select the items that are most closely related to the task you are doing.

Primary and secondary research, and the law of copyright

There are two ways to research information. One is known as primary research, the other is secondary research.

Primary research

Primary research involves finding new information about an issue or topic. This might include finding out people's views about a product or interviewing an expert. When carrying out interviews, you will need to design a survey or questionnaire. Your primary research might also include observing or experiencing something for yourself, and recording your feelings and observations.

Secondary research

Secondary research involves accessing information that already exists in books, files, newspapers or on CD-ROMs, computer databases or the internet, and assessing it against your objectives.

This information has been prepared by other people and is available to anyone. You can quote from an original work provided you acknowledge the source of your information. You should put this acknowledgement in your text or in the bibliography to your text; do not claim it as your own research. You must include the author's name, year of publication, the title and publisher, or the web address if it is an online article. You should practise listing the sources of articles so that you feel confident writing a bibliography. Use the guidance sheet issued by your centre to help you. This will illustrate the style your centre recommends.

The trick with research is to choose the best technique to achieve your objectives and this may mean using a mix of methods and resources. For example, if you have to comment on an industry event you might go to it, make notes, interview people attending, observe the event (perhaps take a video camera), and read any newspaper reports or online comments.

People as a source of information

If you want to get the most out of interviewing someone, or several people, you need to prepare carefully in advance.

The following points give some general advice about getting the most out of face-to-face interviews.

- Make sure you know what questions to ask to get the information you need.
- Explain why you want the information.
- Don't expect to be told confidential or sensitive information.
- Write clear notes so that you remember who told you what, and when. (See also page 68.)
- Note the contact details of the person you are interviewing and ask whether they mind if you contact them again should you think of anything later or need to clarify your notes.
- Thank them for their help.

If you want to ask a lot of people for their opinion you may want to conduct a survey. You will need to design a questionnaire and analyse the results. This will be easier if you ask for **quantitative** responses – for example yes/no, true/false or ratings on a five-point scale – rather than opinions.

- Give careful thought to your representative sample (people whose opinions are relevant to the topic).
- Decide how many people to survey so that the results mean something.
- Keep the survey relatively short.

- Thank people who complete it.
- Analyse the results, and write up your conclusions promptly.

TOP TIP

Test your questionnaire on volunteers before you 'go live' to check that there are no mistakes and the questions are easy to understand. Make any amendments before you conduct your 'real' survey.

Asking someone who knows a lot about a topic can be informative.

Avoiding pitfalls

Wikipedia is a good online source that covers many topics, and often in some depth. It is popular and free. However, it has an open-content policy, which means that anyone can contribute to and edit entries. People may post information, whether it is correct or not. Wikipedia is moving towards greater checks on entries, but it is still sensible to check out information you find on this site somewhere else.

Apart from inaccuracy, you may find other problems with information you obtain through research, especially material found online.

- **Out-of-date material.** Check the date of everything and keep only the latest version of books, newspapers or magazines. Yesterday's news may be of little use if you are researching something topical.
- **Irrelevant details.** Often, only part of an article will be relevant to your search. For example, if you are forecasting future trends in an area of work, you do not need information about its history or related problems. When learners are struggling, they sometimes 'pad out' answers with irrelevant information. If you've researched properly you can avoid this by having enough relevant information for your purposes.

- **Invalid assumptions.** This means someone has jumped to the wrong conclusion and made 2 + 2 = 5. You might do this if you see two friends chatting and think they are talking about you – whether they are or not! You can avoid problems in this area by double-checking your ideas and getting evidence to support them.

- **Bias.** This is when people hold strong views about a topic, or let their emotions or prejudices affect their judgement. An obvious example is asking a keen football fan for an objective evaluation of their team's performance!

- **Vested interests.** People may argue in a certain way because it's in their own interests to do so. For example, when the Government said Home Information Packs must be prepared for all properties being sold, the Association of Home Information Pack Providers was in favour because it trains the people who prepare the packs. The National Association of Estate Agents and Royal Institution of Chartered Surveyors were not because they thought they would lose business if people were put off selling their houses.

TOP TIP

Don't discard information that is affected by bias or vested interests. Just make it clear you know about the problem and have taken it into account.

Reading for a purpose

You may enjoy reading or you may find it tedious or difficult. If so, it helps to know that there are different ways to read, depending on what you're doing. For example, you wouldn't look for a programme in a TV guide in the same way that you would check an assignment for mistakes. You can save time and find information more easily if you use the best method of reading to suit your purpose. The following are some examples of ways of reading.

- **Skim reading** is used to check new information and get a general overview. To skim a book chapter read the first and last paragraphs, the headings, subheadings and illustrations. It also helps to read the first sentence of each paragraph.

TOP TIP

News articles are written with the key points at the beginning, so concentrate on the first paragraph or two. Feature articles have a general introduction and important information is contained in the main text.

- **Scanning** is used to see whether an article contains something you need – such as key words, dates or technical terms. Focus on capital or initial letters for a name, and figures for a date. Technical terms may be in bold or italics.

- **Light reading** is usually done for pleasure when you are relaxed, for example, reading a magazine article. You may not remember many facts afterwards, so this sort of reading isn't suitable for learning something or assessing its value.

- **Word-by-word reading (proofreading)** is important so that you don't miss anything, such as the dosage instructions for a strong medicine. You should proofread assignments before you submit them.

- **Reading for study (active reading)** means being actively involved so that you understand the information. It is rare to be naturally good at this, so you might have to work to develop this skill.

Developing critical and analytical skills

Developing critical and analytical skills involves looking at information for any flaws in the arguments. These skills are important when you progress to work or higher education (HE), so it's useful to practise them now on your BTEC Level 3 National course.

A useful technique for understanding, analysing, evaluating and remembering what you are reading is **SQ4R**.

SQ4R is an effective method. It consists of six steps.

1 Survey first, to get a general impression. Scan the information to see what it is about, when it was written and by whom. The source, and the reason it was written, may be important. Most newspapers, for example, have their own 'slant' that affects how information is presented.

2 Question your aims for reading this material. What are you hoping to find? What questions are you expecting it to answer?

3 Read the information three or four times. The first time, aim to get a general idea of the content. Use a dictionary to look up any new words. Then read more carefully to really understand what the writer means.

4 Respond by thinking critically about the information and how it relates to the topic you are studying. Does it answer your queries partially, fully or not at all? What information is factual and what is based on opinion? Is there evidence to support these opinions? Is there a reason why the author has taken this standpoint? Do you agree with it? How does it link to other information you have read? What is the opposite argument and is there any evidence to support this? Overall, how useful is this information?

5 Record the information by noting the key points. Use this to refresh your memory, if necessary, rather than re-reading the article.

6 Review your notes against the original to check you have included all important points. If you are also preparing a presentation, reviewing your notes will help you to remember key points more easily.

TOP TIP

SQ4R is just one method of reading for study. Research others and adapt them to suit your own style.

Taking good notes

There are many occasions when you need to take notes, such as when a visiting speaker is talking to your class. There's no point taking notes unless you write them in a way that will allow you to use them later.

Note-taking is a personal activity. Some people prefer to make diagrammatical sketches with key points in boxes linked by arrows; others prefer to write a series of bullet points. You will develop your own style, but the following hints and tips might help you at the start.

- Use A4 lined paper, rather than a notebook, so that you have more space and don't need to turn over so often.
- When you're reading for study, make sure you have a dictionary, pen, notepad and highlighter to hand.
- Leave a wide margin to record your own comments or queries.
- Put a heading at the top, such as the speaker's name and topic, as well as the date.
- If you are making notes from a book or an article, remember SQ4R and read it several times first. Your notes will only be effective if you understand the information.
- Don't write in complete sentences – it takes too long.
- Leave spaces for later additions or corrections.
- Use headings to keep your notes clear and well organised.
- Only write down relevant information, including key words and phrases.

- Highlight, underline or use capitals for essential points.
- Never copy chunks of text — always use your own words.
- Clearly identify quotations, and record your sources, so that you can cite them in your work. (Note the author's name, title, publisher, date and place of publication and the page number.)

TOP TIP

Make sure your information is accurate, up-to-date, relevant and valid. Be aware of bias, and don't confuse fact with opinion.

Key points

- Useful information may be verbal, printed, written, graphical or electronic.
- Effective research means knowing exactly what you are trying to find and where to look. Know how reference media are stored in your library and how to search online. Store important information carefully.
- Primary research is original data you obtain yourself. Secondary research is information prepared by someone else. If you use this, you must quote your sources in a bibliography.
- You can search for information by skimming and scanning, and read in different ways. Reading for study means actively involving yourself with the text, questioning what you are reading and making notes to help your own understanding.
- Read widely around a topic to get different viewpoints. Don't accept everything you read as correct. Think about how it fits with other information you have obtained.
- Taking notes is a personal skill that takes time to develop. Start by using A4 lined pages with a margin, set out your notes clearly and label them. Only record essential information.

Action points

- Working with a friend, look back at the sources of information listed on page 64. For each type, identify examples of information relevant to your course that you could obtain from each source. See how many you can list under each type.
- Check your ability to find the information you need by answering each of the questions in **Activity: Finding information** on the next page. For any questions you get wrong, your first research task is to find out the correct answers as quickly as you can.
- Go to page 96 to find out how to access a website where you can check your ability to skim and scan information, improve your ability to differentiate fact from opinion, summarise text and much more.
- Check your ability to sort fact from opinion and spot vested interests by completing **Activity: Let's give you a tip...** on page 72. Check your ideas with the answers on page 95.

TOP TIP

Make a note of any information that you are struggling to understand so that you can discuss it with your tutor.

Activity: Finding information

Answer the following questions about finding information.

a) Four types of information that are available from the library in your centre, besides books, are:

1

2

3

4

b) When I visit the library, the way to check if a book I want is available is:

c) The difference between borrowing a book on short-term loan and on long-term loan is:

Short-term loan:

Long-term loan:

d) The journals that are stocked by the library that are relevant to my course include:

e) Useful information on the intranet at my centre includes:

f) Searchable databases and online magazines I can access include:

g) The quickest way to check if a book or journal contains the type of information I need is to:

_____

_____

h) The difference between a search engine, a portal, a directory site and a forum is:

_____

_____

i) Bookmarking useful websites means:

_____

_____

j) In addition to suggesting websites, Google can also provide the following types of information.

_____

_____

k) Specialist websites which provide useful information related to my course include:

_____

_____

l) Useful tips I would give to people starting on my course who need to find out information are:

_____

_____

_____

Activity: Let's give you a tip...

In 2009, many businesses were struggling thanks to the credit crunch and falling consumer demand. Some, like Woolworths, closed down altogether. Others laid off staff, or announced wage cuts. Despite this, the Government approved recommendations by the Low Pay Commission to increase the minimum wage rate from October. Although the rise was only small, many unions, including Unison and Usdaw, agreed it was better than a freeze, which had been wanted by the British Chambers of Commerce and the British Retail Consortium.

The Government also announced new laws to stop restaurants and bars using tips to top up staff pay to the minimum level. *The Independent* newspaper claimed its 'fair tips, fair pay' campaign had won the day. It also reported that the British Hospitality Association was claiming this could result in up to 45,000 job losses. The Unite union also carried out a campaign and its General Secretary claimed the decision a triumph for the poorly paid. Not everyone agreed. Some thought there should be no tipping at all, as in Australia. Others said the Canadian system was best – wages are low but generous tips are left, and this motivates staff to give excellent service.

a) Look at the table below. In your view, which of the statements are facts and which are opinions? In each case, justify your view.

Statement	Fact or opinion?	Justification
i) Having a national minimum wage helps low-paid workers.		
ii) Over one million people will benefit from the minimum wage increase.		
iii) The new law on tips will stop restaurants paying below minimum wage rates.		
iv) Using the Australian system of no tips would be better.		
v) The Canadian system guarantees good service.		
vi) 45,000 job losses will occur in the hospitality industry.		

b) All newspapers have their own way of putting forward the news. Go to page 96 to find out how you can access a website which will help you to compare the way that news is reported in different newspapers.

Compare six different newspapers and make notes on:

i) the type of stories covered

ii) the way views are put forward

Activity: In your own words

Read this article and attempt to reword its main points in your own words. You can also directly quote a small section of it:

Got some strange emails from your friends recently? If you have, chances are their accounts have been hacked. Just when you thought Cyber Security couldn't get any scarier, news has recently broken that around 30,000 account log-on details have been stolen from Yahoo!, Hotmail, Gmail and other web-based mail services.

How can this happen? Users were probably tricked into visiting fake websites and entering their log-in details, thinking that they were using the authentic home page of the email provider. Yet another example of a phishing attack. The worrying thing is that, despite all the investment in teaching users about security, they can still be fooled into entering their log-in credentials on fake websites and criminals can make money by selling these account details to spammers. Our confidence in the security of the online world will be severely damaged unless a solution can be found to this problem.

Phishing is a difficult problem to combat because many of the suggested solutions will compromise the convenience of the internet – the very thing which makes it so popular. The best solution would probably be continuing work to educate users so that they better understand how online services work and so they can make sensible and informed decisions about which sites to trust and which they should be wary of.

Whatever the solution, the problem doesn't look like it will go away any time soon and, by the look of things, it will get worse. So watch out for more strange advertising emails from your friends.

Step Nine: Make an effective presentation

Case study: Effective preparation for presentations

Giving presentations is an important element of your BTEC course. It can be split into two main areas, both of which require different and significant skills. Firstly, preparing the presentation and the material you will use to support it. Usually, the support material will consist of a set of slides created in a presentation program like PowerPoint. The second area is actually giving the presentation, which requires different, but equally important skills.

Rashad has not done many presentations before, so when he sees that one of the assignment tasks for Unit 4: Impact of the Use of IT on Business Systems is to do a presentation on how to improve a business system using IT, he feels a bit apprehensive. He wants to do well in this assignment so he spends a lot of time researching the required information and creating presentation slides. He decides that the best plan is to put all the information he has onto the slides. He ends up with 20 slides, all packed with lots of detailed information.

When it comes to giving the presentation he feels very nervous. Standing at the front, with everyone looking at him, he reads through the information on each slide. After the fifth slide the teacher tells him he has to stop as each student is only allocated 10 minutes for their presentation and he has already taken 15 minutes. Rashad had not noticed this limit when he read the assignment. The feedback he gets from the teacher about his presentation is not good and he is keen to know how he could improve next time.

Reflection points

What mistakes do you think Rashad made in preparing his presentation?

What steps do you think Rashad could take to do well in his next presentation?

Making a presentation can be nerve-wracking. It involves several skills, including planning, preparation and communication. It tests your ability to work in a team, speak in public and use IT (normally PowerPoint). You also have to stay calm under pressure. However, as it is excellent practice for your future, you can expect presentations to be a common method of assessing your performance.

TOP TIP

When you're giving a presentation, keep to time, get to the point and use your time well.

You will give better presentations if you note the following points.

Good planning and preparation

Being well prepared, and rehearsing beforehand, helps your confidence and your presentation. The following points will help you to do this.

- If you're part of a team, find out everyone's strengths and weaknesses and divide work fairly taking these into account. Decide how long each person should speak, who should introduce the team and who will summarise at the end.

- Take into account your time-scale, resources and team skills. A simple, clear presentation is better – and safer – than a complicated one.

- If you're using PowerPoint, make slides more interesting by avoiding a series of bulleted lists and including artwork. Print PowerPoint notes for the audience. Use a fuller set of notes for yourself, as a prompt.

- Check the venue and time.

- Decide what to wear and check it's clean and presentable.

- Prepare, check and print your handouts.

- Decide, as a team, the order in which people will speak, bearing in mind the topic.

- Discuss possible questions and how to answer them.

- Rehearse beforehand to check your timings.

If you prepare properly you can really enjoy giving a presentation.

TOP TIP

Rehearsing properly allows you to speak fluently, just glancing at your notes to remind you of the next key point.

On the day, you can achieve a better performance if you:

- arrive in plenty of time
- calm your nerves by taking deep breaths before going in front of your audience
- introduce yourself clearly, and smile at the audience
- avoid reading from your screen or your notes
- explain what you are going to do – especially if giving a demonstration – do it and then review what you've done
- say you will deal with questions at the end of any demonstration
- answer questions honestly – don't exaggerate, guess or waffle
- respond positively to all feedback, which should be used to improve your performance next time.

TOP TIP

Make sure you can be heard clearly by lifting your head and speaking a little more slowly and loudly than normal.

Key points

- When making a presentation, prepare well, don't be too ambitious and have several rehearsals.
- When giving a demonstration, explain first what you are going to do and that you will answer questions at the end.

Case study: Learner quotes about making presentations

Most people start off feeling uncomfortable about talking in front of a group of people, whether they know them or not. This is what some real learners have said about having to give presentations as part of their BTEC course.

"I actually feel more comfortable giving a presentation rather than having to write an essay. What I really enjoy about it is the fact that sometimes we have to prepare a presentation as a whole group. I like that we work together to find information and then we take turns presenting different points. The fact that I am not the only one out there and I am part of a supportive team makes it fun for me."

Gabriela, 16, BTEC Level 2 First in Performing Arts

"Although presentations are very stressful, when I present my work it helps to hang my ideas together and I find I can express what I want to say more clearly than when I write things down. Instant feedback is helpful and boosts my confidence for the next time."

Ethan, 19, BTEC Level 2 First in Creative Media Production

"I think presentations are useful but I find them difficult to deliver – relying heavily on my memory, which is very nerve-racking. We were told that presentation would be part of our assessment. I really worried about it and couldn't sleep the night before – stressing out about what I was going to say. I hated the first few minutes, but after that I was OK."

Will, 16, BTEC Level 2 First in Engineering

"I was very nervous about presenting to my class until I took part in the Young Enterprise scheme and had to present the results of our project to over 200 people including the mayor! After that, presenting to my class mates didn't feel too nerve-wracking at all."

Lizzy, 17, BTEC Level 2 First in Business

"I used to dread presentations on my course, but found that if I went through my notes again and again until I knew the presentation inside out, it made it much easier and the presentations generally went well."

Javinder, 17, BTEC Level 3 National in Construction

"I used to hate presenting to other people on my course, until I realised that most of them were as nervous about it as I was!"

Koichi, 21, BTEC Level 3 National in Art and Design

Activity: All right on the night?

Read the following account and answer the questions that follow. If possible, compare ideas with a friend in your class.

Gemma looked around in exasperation. The team were on the final rehearsal of their presentation and nothing was going right. Amaya seemed to think it was funny. 'Honestly, Gemma, why don't you just chill for a bit?' she suggested. 'You know what they say – a bad dress rehearsal means we'll do really well tomorrow!'

Gemma glared at her. 'Well, can I make a suggestion, too, Amaya,' she retorted. 'Why don't you just concentrate for a change? Sprawling around and dissolving into giggles every five minutes isn't helping either.'

She turned to Adam. 'And I thought you were going to build a simple model,' she said, 'not one that falls apart every time you touch it.'

Adam looked crest-fallen. 'But I wanted to show how it worked.'

'How it's supposed to work, you mean!' raged Gemma, all her worries and anxieties now coming to the fore. 'We'll look stupid if it ends up in bits on the floor tomorrow and Amaya just falls about laughing again.'

'And Imran,' continued Gemma, turning her sights on the last member of the team, 'why is it so difficult for you to count to three minutes? We've agreed over and over again we'll each talk for three minutes and every time you get carried away with the sound of your own voice and talk for twice as long. It just means we're going to overrun and get penalised. And stop trying to wriggle out of answering questions properly. For heaven's sake, if you don't know the answer, how hard is it just to say so?'

Silence fell. No-one looked at each other. Adam fiddled with his model and something else fell off. Amaya wanted to laugh but didn't dare.

Imran was sulking and vowed never to say anything ever again. 'You wait,' he thought. 'Tomorrow I'll race through my part in one minute flat. And then what are you going to do?'

1 Identify the strengths and weaknesses of each member of the presentation team.

Name	Strengths	Weaknesses
Gemma		
Amaya		
Adam		
Imran		

2 What have the team done right, so far, in getting ready for their presentation?

3 Why do you think they are having problems?

4 If you were Gemma's tutor, what advice would you give her at this point?

Activity: Presentation – running your own business

Many young people have aspirations to run their own business. Think about:

- What kind of business you would like to run.
- How that business would work.
- What product or service you would sell.
- How you would market your business to potential customers.
- How you would use IT to support your business.

Unit 3: Information Systems is about how IT supports business processes.

Create a presentation about the business you would like to set up and run and how your business will use IT to collect and manipulate information.

Plan your presentation here.

Introduction – about my business
How I would market (advertise) my product or service
How I would sell and deliver my product and service
How I would use IT to support my business
Information I would collect and process using IT
Summary

TOP TIP

When making presentations using PowerPoint, don't just read out what it says on the slides. The audience can do this. Use the slides as prompt cards.

Step Ten: Maximise your opportunities and manage your problems

Case study: Tackling problems

Silvia and Aidan are two students facing problems. Silvia has problems at home, and this has resulted in her missing some lessons. She finds it very difficult to work at home and the situation has made it difficult to concentrate in class. She doesn't really want to trouble her tutor with all her problems so doesn't tell her much about what is going on. When the tutor asks why she is missing classes and is so behind with her assignments she just gives vague excuses about her home situation. She certainly doesn't want to go into detail. In the end she just avoids her tutor as much as possible even though she keeps phoning her and even writes a letter home. After Christmas she feels that there is no point continuing as she is so far behind with her assignments so she leaves the course.

Aidan has problems as, a few weeks after starting the course, he becomes ill. He has to go and see his GP quite a few times and also visit the hospital for tests. Each time he is off or late he phones his college to let them know. He also books an appointment with his tutor to discuss the situation as he is worried about all the lessons he is missing. His tutor is understanding and arranges for all the materials for lessons he has missed to be emailed to him.

Aidan is then told that he needs an operation so, again, he speaks to his tutor who arranges extensions for his upcoming assignments. After the operation Aidan needs several weeks at home to recover but when he feels well enough he is able to read through the lesson materials that have been emailed to him. After Christmas he is feeling a lot better but he is worried about his course as he has missed so much. He has another meeting with his tutor and some extra 'catch up' workshops are arranged for him. Aidan and his tutor agree an extension for the assignments due after Christmas. It is hard work catching up with all the missing work but Aidan's tutor is very sympathetic and gives him as much extra help as possible. By Easter he has completed all the outstanding assignments and is back on track.

Reflection points

If you were in Aidan or Sylvia's position, how would you tackle your problem?

Why do you think it is important to talk to your tutor as soon as possible if you have an issue or problem you need to discuss?

If your course takes one or two years to complete, then it is highly likely that you will experience some highs and lows in that time. You may find one or two topics harder than the rest. There may be distractions in your personal life to cope with. All of which means than you may not always be able to do your best.

It is, therefore, sensible to have an action plan to help you cope. It's also wise to plan how to make the best of opportunities for additional experiences or learning. This section shows you how to do this.

TOP TIP

Because life rarely runs smoothly, it's sensible to capitalise on the opportunities that come your way and have a plan to deal with problems.

Making the most of your opportunities

There will be many opportunities for learning on your course, not all of which will be in school or college. You should prepare for some of the following to maximise the opportunities that each offer.

- **External visits**. Prepare in advance by reading about relevant topics. Make notes when you are there. Write up your notes neatly and file them safely for future reference.

- **Visiting speakers**. Questions can usually be submitted to the speaker in advance. Think carefully about information that you would find helpful. Make notes, unless someone has been appointed to make notes for the whole group. You may be asked to thank the speaker on behalf of your group.

- **Work experience**. If work experience is an essential part of your course, your tutor will help you to organise your placement and tell you about the evidence you need to obtain. You may also get a special logbook in which to record your experiences. Read and re-read the units to which your evidence will apply and make sure you understand the grading criteria and what you need to obtain. Make time to write up your notes, logbook and/or diary every night (if possible), while everything is fresh in your mind.

- **In your own workplace**. If you have a full-time or part-time job, watch for opportunities to find out more about relevant topics that relate to your course, such as health and safety, teamwork, dealing with customers, IT security and communications. Your employer will have had to address all of these issues. Finding out more about these issues will broaden your knowledge and give more depth to your assessment responses.

- **Television, newspapers, podcasts and other information sources**. The media can be an invaluable source of information. Look out for news bulletins relating to your studies, as well as information in topical television programmes – from *The Apprentice* to *Top Gear*. You can also read news headlines online. Podcasts are useful, too. It will help if you know what topics you will be studying in the months to come, so you can spot useful opportunities as they arise.

TOP TIP

Remember that you can use online catch-up services, such as the BBC iPlayer or 4oD (for Channel 4 shows) to see TV programmes you have missed recently.

Minimising problems

Hopefully, any problems you experience during your course will only be minor; such as struggling to find an acceptable working method with someone in your team.

You should already know who to talk to about these issues, and who to go to if that person is absent or you would prefer to talk to someone else. If your problems are affecting your work, it's sensible to see your tutor promptly. It is a rare learner who is enthusiastic about every topic and gets on well with everyone else doing the course, so your tutor won't be surprised and will give you useful guidance (in confidence) to help.

TOP TIP

Don't delay talking to someone in confidence if you have a serious problem. If your course tutor is unavailable, talk to another staff member you like and trust.

Other sources of help

If you are unfortunate enough to have a more serious personal problem, the following sources of help may be available in your centre.

- **Professional counselling.** There may be a professional counselling service. If you see a counsellor, nothing you say during the session can be mentioned to another member of staff without your permission.

- **Complaint procedures.** If you have a serious complaint, the first step is to talk to your tutor. If you can't resolve your problem informally, there will be a formal learner complaint procedure. These procedures are used only for serious issues, not for minor difficulties.

- **Appeals procedures.** If you disagree with your final grade for an assignment, check the grading criteria and ask the subject tutor to explain how the grade was awarded. If you are still unhappy, talk to your personal tutor. If you still disagree, you have the right to make a formal appeal.

- **Disciplinary procedures.** These exist for when learners consistently flout a centre's rules and ensure that all learners are dealt with in the same way. Hopefully, you will never get into trouble, but you should make sure that you read these procedures carefully to see what could happen if you did. Remember that being honest and making a swift apology is always the wisest course of action.

- **Serious illness.** Whether this involves you, a family member or a close friend, it could affect your attendance. Discuss the problem with your tutor promptly; you will be missing information from the first day you are absent. There are many solutions in this type of situation – such as sending notes by post and updating you electronically (providing you are well enough to cope with the work).

TOP TIP

It's important to know your centre's procedures for dealing with important issues such as complaints, major illnesses, learner appeals and disciplinary matters.

Key points

- Don't miss opportunities to learn more about relevant topics through external visits, listening to visiting speakers, work experience, being at work or even watching television.

- If you have difficulties or concerns, talk to your tutor, or another appropriate person, promptly to make sure your work isn't affected.

Action points

1 Prepare in advance to maximise your opportunities.
   a) List the opportunities available on your course for obtaining more information and talking to experts. You can check with your tutor to make sure you've identified them all.
   b) Check the content of each unit you will be studying so that you know the main topics and focus of each.
   c) Identify the information that may be relevant to your course on television, on radio, in newspapers and in podcasts.

2 Make sure you know how to cope if you have a serious problem.
   a) Check your centre's procedures so you know who to talk to in a crisis, and who to contact if that person is absent.
   b) Find out where you can get hold of a copy of the main procedures in your centre that might affect you if you have a serious problem. Then read them.

Activity: Sources of help

There are lots of different places you can go and people you can speak to who can help you deal with any problems you have during the course. Some of these are informal sources like your friends and family, others are more formal sources provided by your school or college and by Edexcel. You can use the table below to make a list of the contact details of various people who may be able to help you with problems.

Source of help/information	Telephone number	Email address/website
Tutor or head of year		
School or college department office		
Careers advisor		
Youth worker/counsellor		
Edexcel		
Student union		
Learning advisor		
Student class representative		
Connexions		

AND FINALLY ...

Refer to this Study Skills Guide whenever you need to remind yourself about something related to your course. Keep it in a safe place so that you can use it whenever you need to refresh your memory. That way, you'll get the very best out of your course – and yourself!

Your Study Skills Guide will help you gain the skills you need for success.

Skills building

This section has been written to help you improve the skills needed to do your best in your assignments. You may be excellent at some skills already, others may need further work. The skills you can expect to demonstrate on your course include:

- your personal, learning and thinking skills (**PLTS**)
- your **functional skills** of ICT, maths/numeracy and English
- your proofreading and document production skills.

Personal, learning and thinking skills (PLTS)

These are the skills, personal qualities and behaviour that enable you to operate more independently, work more confidently with other people and be more effective at work. You'll develop these on your BTEC Level 3 National course through a variety of experiences and as you take on different roles and responsibilities.

The skills are divided into six groups:

1 **Independent enquirers** can process and evaluate information they investigate from different perspectives. They can plan what to do and how to do it, and take into account the consequences of making different decisions.

2 **Creative thinkers** generate and explore different ideas. They make connections between ideas, events and experiences that enable them to be inventive and imaginative.

3 **Reflective learners** can assess themselves and other people. They can evaluate their own strengths and limitations. They set themselves realistic goals, monitor their own performance and welcome feedback.

4 **Team workers** collaborate with other people to achieve common goals. They are fair and considerate to others, whether as a team leader or team member, and take account of different opinions.

5 **Self-managers** are well-organised and show personal responsibility, initiative, creativity and enterprise. They look for new challenges and responsibilities and are flexible when priorities change.

6 **Effective participators** play a full part in the life of their school, college, workplace or wider community by taking responsible action to bring improvements for others as well as themselves.

Action points

1 Many parts of this Study Skills Guide relate to the development of your own personal, learning and thinking skills. For each of the following, suggest the main skill groups to which the chapter relates. Refer to the box above and write a number next to each chapter title below.

a) Use your time wisely. _____

b) Understand how to research and analyse information. _____

c) Work productively as a member of a group. _____

d) Understand yourself. _____

e) Utilise all your resources. _____

f) Maximise your opportunities and manage your problems. _____

2 You have been on your BTEC National course for a few months now and, although everyone is enjoying the work, you realise that some of the learners have complaints.

Firstly, several learners object to an increase in the price of printouts and photocopying, on the basis that they can't do good work for their assignments if this is too expensive. You disagree and think that the prices are reasonable, given the cost of paper.

Secondly, a timetable change means your 2 pm – 4 pm Friday afternoon class has been moved to 9 am – 11 am. Some learners are annoyed and want it changed back, while others are delighted.

a) For the first problem, identify four factors which could indicate that those complaining about the price rise might be justified.

1

2

3

4

b) For the second problem:

  i) Think about which learners in your group would be most affected by the timetable change. Who might be most disturbed? Who might benefit from the earlier start?

  ii) Try to think of a creative solution, or compromise, that would please both groups.

c) During the discussions about these issues, some quieter members of the class are often shouted down by the more excitable members. Suggest a strategy for dealing with this, which everyone is likely to accept.

You can also check your ideas with the suggestions given on page 95.

3 a) Complete the chart opposite, identifying occasions when you may need to demonstrate personal, learning and thinking skills in your future career. Alternatively, apply each area to a part-time job you are currently doing.

b) Identify areas where you think you are quite strong and put a tick in the 'S' column. Check that you could provide evidence to support this judgement, such as a time when you have demonstrated this skill.

c) Now consider areas where you are not so good and put a cross in the 'W' column.

d) Then practise self-management by identifying two appropriate goals to achieve over the next month and make a note of them in the space provided. If possible, talk through your ideas at your next individual tutorial.

Personal, learning and thinking skills for future career/current part-time job				
Skill group	Example skills	Occasions when you use/ will use skill	S	W
Independent enquirers	Finding information Solving problems Making decisions Reconciling conflicting information or views Justifying decisions			
Creative thinkers	Finding imaginative solutions Making original connections Finding new ways to do something Opportunities for being innovative and inventive			
Reflective learners	Goals you may set yourself Reviewing your own progress Encouraging feedback Dealing with setbacks or criticism			
Team workers	Working with others Coping with different views to your own Adapting your behaviour Being fair and considerate			
Self-managers	Being self-starting and showing initiative Dealing positively with changing priorities Organising your own time and resources Dealing with pressure Managing your emotions			
Effective participators	Identifying issues of concern to others Proposing ways forward Identifying improvements for others Influencing other people Putting forward a persuasive argument			
Goals	1			
	2			

Functional skills

Functional skills are practical skills that everyone needs to have in order to study and work effectively. They involve using and applying English, maths and ICT.

Improving your literacy skills

Your written English communication skills

A good vocabulary increases your ability to explain yourself clearly. Work that is presented without spelling and punctuation errors looks professional, and increases the likelihood of someone understanding your intended meaning. Your written communication skills will be tested in many assignments. You should work at improving areas of weakness, such as spelling, punctuation or vocabulary.

Try the following to help you improve your written communication skills:

- Read more as this introduces you to new words, and it will help your spelling.
- Look up new words in a dictionary and try to use them in conversation.
- Use a Thesaurus (you can access one electronically in Word) to find alternatives to words you use a lot, this adds variety to your work.
- Never use words you don't understand in the hope that they sound impressive.
- Write neatly, so people can read what you've written.
- Do crosswords to improve your word power and spelling.
- Improve your punctuation – especially the use of apostrophes – either by using an online programme or by using a communication textbook.
- See page 96 to gain access to some helpful websites.

Verbal and non–verbal communication (NVC) skills

Talking appropriately means using the right words and 'tone'; using the right body language means sending positive signals to reinforce this message – such as smiling at someone when you say 'Hello'. Both verbal and non-verbal communication skills are essential when dealing with people at work.

The following are some hints for successful communication:

- Be polite, tactful and sensitive to other people's feelings.
- Think about the words and phrases that you like to hear, and use them when communicating with other people.
- Use simple language so that people can understand you easily. Explain what you mean, when necessary.
- Speak at the right pace. Don't speak so slowly that everyone loses interest, or so fast that no-one can understand you.
- Speak loudly enough for people to hear you clearly – but don't shout!
- Think about the specific needs of different people – whether you are talking to a senior manager, an important client, a shy colleague or an angry customer.
- Recognise the importance of non-verbal communication (NVC) so that you send positive signals by smiling, making eye contact, giving an encouraging nod or leaning forwards to show interest.
- Read other people's body language to spot if they are anxious or impatient so that you can react appropriately.

TOP TIP

Make sure you use the right tone for the person you're talking to. Would you talk to an adult in the same way you'd talk to a very young child?

Action points

1 Go to page 96 to see how to gain access to websites which can help you to improve your literacy skills.

2 A battery made in China contained the following information.

> **DO NOT CONNECT IMPROPERLY**
>
> **CHARGE OR DISPOSE OF IN FIRE**

a) Can you see any problems with this? Give a reason for your answer.

b) Reword the information so that it is unambiguous.

3 If you ever thought you could completely trust the spellchecker on your computer, type the text given in box A on the next page into your computer. Your spellchecker will not highlight a single error; yet even at a glance you should be able to spot dozens of errors!

Read the passage in box A and try to understand it. Then rewrite it in box B on the next page without spelling, grammatical or punctuation errors. Compare your finished work with the suggested version on page 95.

Box A

Anyone desirable to write books or reports, be they short or long, should strive too maximise they're optimal use of one's English grammar and obliviously there is an need for correct spelling two one should not neglect punctuation neither.

Frequent lea, many people and individuals become confusing or just do not no it, when righting, when words that mean different, when sounding identically, or when pronounced very similar, are knot too bee spelled inn the same whey. The quay two suck seeding is dew care, a lack off witch Leeds too Miss Spellings that mite otherwise of bean a voided. Spell chequers donut find awl missed takes.

Despite all the pitfalls how ever, with practise, patients and the right altitude, any one can soon become a grate writer and speaker, as what I did.

Box B Now rewrite the passage in the space below without errors.

4 In each of the statements listed in the table below suggest what the body language described might mean.

Statement	What might this body language mean?
a) You are talking to your manager when he steps away from you and crosses his arms over his chest.	
b) You are talking to your friend about what she did at the weekend but she's avoiding making eye contact with you.	
c) During a tutorial session, your tutor is constantly tapping his fingers on the arm of his chair.	
d) Whenever you talk to your friend about your next assignment, she bites her lower lip.	

Improving your maths or numeracy skills

If you think numeracy isn't relevant to you, then think again! Numeracy is an essential life skill. If you can't carry out basic calculations accurately then you will have problems, perhaps when you least expect them. You'll often encounter numbers in various contexts – sometimes they will be correctly given, sometimes not. Unless you have a basic understanding about numeracy, you won't be able to tell the difference.

Good numeracy skills will improve your ability to express yourself, especially in assignments and at work. If you have problems, there are strategies that you can practise to help:

- Try to do basic calculations in your head, then check them on a calculator.

- Ask your tutor for help if important calculations give you problems.

- When you are using your computer, use the onscreen calculator (or a spreadsheet package) to do calculations.

- Investigate puzzle sites and brain training software, such as Dr Kageyama's Maths Training by Nintendo.

Action points

1   Go to page 96 to find out how to gain access to websites which can help you to improve your numeracy skills.

2   Try the following task with a friend or family member.

   Each of you should write down 36 simple calculations in a list, eg 8 × 6, 19 – 8, 14 + 6.

   Exchange lists. See who can answer the most calculations correctly in the shortest time.

3   Figures aren't always what they appear to be. For example, Sophie watches *Who Wants To Be A Millionaire?* She hears Chris Tarrant say that there have been over 500 shows, with 1200 contestants who have each won over £50,000 on average. Five people have won £1 million.

Sophie says she is going to enter because she is almost certain to win more than £50,000 and could even win a million pounds.

a) On the figures given, what is the approximate total of money won over 500 shows (to the nearest £ million)?

b) Assuming that Sophie is chosen to appear on the show, and makes it on air as a contestant, do you think Sophie's argument that she will 'almost certainly' win more than £50,000 is correct? Give a reason for your answer. (The correct answer is on page 96.)

4   You have a part-time job and have been asked to carry out a survey on the usage of the drinks vending machine. You decide to survey 500 people, and find that:

- 225 use the machine to buy one cup of coffee per day only

- 100 use the machine to buy one cup of tea per day only

- 75 use the machine to buy one cup of cold drink per day only

- 50 use the machine to buy one cup of hot chocolate per day only

- the rest are non-users

- the ratio of male to female users is 2:1.

a) How many men in your survey use the machine?

b) How many women in your survey use the machine?

c) Calculate the proportion of the people in your survey that use the machine. Express this as a fraction and as a percentage.

d) What is the ratio of coffee drinkers to tea drinkers in your survey?

e) What is the ratio of coffee drinkers to hot chocolate drinkers in your survey?

f) If people continue to purchase from the machine in the same ratio found in your survey, and last month 1800 cups of coffee were sold, what would you expect the sales of the cold drinks to be?

g) Using the answer to **f)**, if coffee costs 65p and all cold drinks cost 60p, how much would have been spent in total last month on these two items?

Improving your ICT skills

Good ICT skills are an asset in many aspects of your daily life and not just for those studying to be IT practitioners.

The following are ways in which you can Improve your ICT skills:

- Check that you can use the main features of the software packages you need to produce your assignments, eg Word, Excel and PowerPoint.
- Choose a good search engine and learn to use it properly. For more information, go to page 96 to find out how to access a useful website.
- Developing and using your IT skills enables you to enhance your assignments. This may include learning how to import and export text and artwork from one package to another; taking digital photographs and inserting them into your work and/or creating drawings or diagrams by using appropriate software.

Action points

1 Check your basic knowledge of IT terminology by identifying each of these items on your computer screen:

a) taskbar	**f)** scroll bars
b) toolbar	**g)** status bar
c) title bar	**h)** insertion point
d) menu bar	**i)** maximise/
e) mouse pointer	minimise button.

2 Assess your IT skills by identifying the packages and operations you find easy to use and those that you find more difficult. If you use Microsoft Office products (Word, PowerPoint, Access or Excel) you can find out more about improving your skills online. Go to page 96 to find out how to access a useful website for this Action point.

3 Search the internet to find a useful dictionary of IT terms. Bookmark it for future use. Find out the meaning of any of the following terms that you don't know already:

a) portal

b) cached link

c) home page

d) browser

e) firewall

f) HTML

g) URL

h) cookie

i) hyperlink

j) freeware.

Proofreading and document preparation skills

Improving your keyboard, document production and general IT skills can save you hours of time. When you have good skills, the work you produce will be of a far more professional standard.

- Think about learning to touch type. Your centre may have a workshop you can join, or you can use an online program – go to page 96 to find out how to access a useful website that will allow you to test and work on improving your typing skills.

- Obtain correct examples of any document formats you will have to use, such as a report or summary, either from your tutor, the internet or from a textbook.

- Proofread all your work carefully. A spellchecker won't find all your mistakes, so you must read through it yourself as well.

- Make sure your work looks professional by using a suitable typeface and font size, as well as reasonable margins.

- Print your work and store the printouts neatly, so that it stays in perfect condition for when you hand it in.

Action points

1 You can check and improve your typing skills using online typing sites – see link in previous section.

2 Check your ability to create documents by scoring yourself out of 5 for each of the following questions, where 5 is something you can do easily and 0 is something you can't do at all. Then focus on improving every score where you rated yourself 3 or less.

I know how to:

a) create a new document and open a saved document _____

b) use the mouse to click, double-click and drag objects _____

c) use drop-down menus _____

d) customise my toolbars by adding or deleting options _____

e) save and/or print a document _____

f) create folders and sub-folders to organise my work _____

g) move a folder I use regularly to My Places _____

h) amend text in a document _____

i) select, copy, paste and delete information in a document _____

j) quickly find and replace text in a document _____

k) insert special characters _____

l) create a table or insert a diagram in a document _____

m) change the text size, font and colour _____

n) add bold, italics or underscore _____

o) create a bullet or numbered list _____

p) align text left, right or centred _____

q) format pages before they are printed _____

r) proofread a document so that there are no mistakes _____.

Answers

Activity: Let's give you a tip... (page 72)

a) i) Fact

ii) Opinion – the number cannot be validated

iii) Fact

iv) Opinion

v) Opinion

vi) Opinion – again the number is estimated

Skills building answers

PLTS Action points (page 85)

1 a) Use your time wisely = **5** Self-managers

b) Understand how to research and analyse information = **1** Independent enquirers, **5** Self-managers

c) Work productively as a member of a group = **4** Team workers, **6** Effective participators

d) Understand yourself = **3** Reflective learners

e) Utilise all your resources = **5** Self-managers

f) Maximise your opportunities and manage your problems = **1** Independent enquirers, **2** Creative thinkers, **3** Reflective learners, **5** Self-managers

2 a) Factors to consider in relation to the increased photocopying/printing charges include: the comparative prices charged by other schools/colleges, how often there is a price rise, whether any printing or photocopying at all can be done without charge, whether there are any concessions for special tasks or assignments, the availability of class sets of books/popular library books for loan (which reduces the need for photocopying).

b) i) An earlier start will be more likely to negatively affect those who live further away and who are reliant on public transport, particularly in rural areas. The earlier finish will benefit anyone who has a part-time job that starts on a Friday afternoon or who has after college commitments, such as looking after younger sisters or brothers.

ii) The scope for compromise would depend on whether there are any classes between 11 am and 2 pm on a Friday, whether tutors had any flexibility and whether the new 9 am – 11 am class could be moved to another time or day.

c) One strategy would be to allow discussion for a set time, ensure everyone had spoken, then put the issue to a vote. The leader should prompt suggestions from quieter members by asking people individually what they think.

Literacy skills action points (pages 89–91)

2 a) The statement reads as if it is acceptable to either charge it or dispose of it in fire.

b) Do not connect this battery improperly. Do not recharge it and do not dispose of it in fire.

3 Anyone who wishes to write books or reports, whether short or long, should try to use English grammatically. Obviously there is a need for correct spelling, too. Punctuation should also not be neglected.

Frequently, people confuse words with different meanings when they are writing, especially when these sound identical or very similar, even when they must not be spelled in the same way. The key to succeeding is due care, a lack of which leads to misspellings that might otherwise have been avoided. Spellcheckers do not find all mistakes.

Despite all the pitfalls, however, with practice, patience and the right attitude, anyone can soon become a great writer and speaker, like me.

4 (Possible answers)

a) Stepping backwards and crossing arms across the chest might indicate that your manager is creating a barrier between you and himself. This may be because he is angry with you.

b) Your friend may be feeling guilty about what she did at the weekend, or not confident that you will approve of what she tells you.

c) Your tutor might be frustrated as he has many things to do and so wants the tutorial to finish quickly.

d) Your friend might be anxious about the next assignment or about the time she has to complete it.

Numeracy skills action points (page 92)

3 a) £60 million

b) Sophie's argument is incorrect as £50,000 is an average, i.e. some contestants will win more, but many will win much less. The distribution of prize money is greater at lower amounts because more people win small amounts of money than large amounts – and only five contestants have won the top prize of £1 million.

4 a) 300

b) 150

c) 9/10ths, 90%

d) 225 : 100 (= 45 : 20) = 9 : 4

e) 225 : 50 = 9 : 2

f) 600

g) £1350

Accessing website links

Links to various websites are referred to throughout this BTEC Level 3 National Study Skills Guide. To ensure that these links are up-to-date, that they work and that the sites aren't inadvertently linked to any material that could be considered offensive, we have made the links available on our website: www.pearsonhotlinks.co.uk. When you visit the site search for either the title BTEC Level 3 National Study Skills Guide in IT or ISBN 9781846905650. From here you can gain access to the website links and information on how they can be used to help you with your studies.

Useful terms

Accreditation of Prior Learning (APL)
Some of your previous achievements and experiences may be able to be used to count towards your qualification.

Apprenticeships
Schemes that enable you to work and earn money at the same time as you gain further qualifications (an NVQ award and a technical certificate) and improve your functional skills. Apprentices learn work-based skills relevant to their job role and their chosen industry. See page 96 to find out how to access a website where you can find out more.

Assessment methods
Techniques used to check that your work demonstrates the learning and understanding required for your qualification, such as assignments, case studies and practical tasks.

Assessor
An assessor is the tutor who marks or assesses your work.

Assignment
A complex task or mini-project set to meet specific grading criteria and learning outcomes.

Awarding body
An organisation responsible for devising, assessing and issuing qualifications. The awarding body for all BTEC qualifications is Edexcel.

Credit value
The number of credits attached to your BTEC course. The credit value increases in relation to the length of time you need to complete the course, from 30 credits for a BTEC Level 3 Certificate, 60 credits for a Subsidiary Diploma, 120 credits for a Diploma, up to 180 credits for an Extended Diploma.

Degrees
Higher education qualifications offered by universities and colleges. Foundation degrees take two years to complete; honours degrees may take three years or longer.

Department for Business Innovation and Skills (BIS)
BIS is responsible for further and higher education and skills training, as well as functions related to trade and industry. See page 96 for information on accessing a website to find out more.

Department for Education
The Department for Education is the government department responsible for schools and education, as well as for children's services.

Distance learning
When you learn and/or study for a qualification at home or at work. You communicate with your tutor and/or the centre that organises the course by post, telephone or electronically.

Educational Maintenance Award (EMA)
An EMA is a means-tested award that provides eligible learners under 19, who are studying a full-time course at school or college, with a cash sum of money every week. See page 96 to find out how to access a website where you can find out more.

External verification
Formal checking of the programme by an Edexcel representative that focuses on sampling various assignments to check content, accurate assessment and grading.

Forbidden combinations
There are some qualifications that cannot be taken simultaneously because their content is too similar.

Functional skills
Practical skills in English, maths and ICT that enable people to work confidently, effectively and independently. Level 2 Functional Skills are mapped to the units of BTEC Level 3 National qualifications. They aren't compulsory to achieve on the course, but are of great use.

Grade boundaries
Pre-set points that determine whether you will achieve a pass, merit or distinction as the overall final grade(s) for your qualification.

Grading criteria

The specific evidence you have to demonstrate to obtain a particular grade in the unit.

Grading domains

The main areas of learning that support the learning outcomes. On a BTEC Level 3 National course these are: application of knowledge and understanding; development of practical and technical skills; personal development for occupational roles; application of PLTS and functional skills.

Grading grid

The table in each unit of your qualification specification that sets out what you have to show you can do.

Higher education (HE)

Post-secondary and post-further education, usually provided by universities and colleges.

Higher-level skills

These are skills such as evaluating or critically assessing information. They are more difficult than lower-level skills such as writing a description or making a list. You must be able to demonstrate higher-level skills to achieve a distinction.

Indicative reading

Recommended books and journals whose content is both suitable and relevant for the BTEC unit studied.

Induction

A short programme of events at the start of a course designed to give you essential information, and introduce you to your fellow learners and tutors, so that you can settle down as quickly and easily as possible.

Internal verification

The quality checks carried out by nominated tutors at your school or college to ensure that all assignments are at the right level, cover appropriate learning outcomes and grading criteria, and that all assessors are marking work consistently and to the same standard.

Investors in People (IiP)

A national quality standard that sets a level of good practice for training and developing of people within a business. Participating organisations must demonstrate commitment to achieve the standard.

Learning outcomes

The knowledge and skills you must demonstrate to show that you have effectively learned a unit.

Learning support

Additional help that is available to all learners in a school or college who have learning difficulties or other special needs.

Levels of study

The depth, breadth and complexity of knowledge, understanding and skills required to achieve a qualification, which also determines its level. Level 2 equates to GCSE level and Level 3 equates to A-level. As you successfully achieve one level, you can then progress to the next. BTEC qualifications are offered at Entry Level, then Levels 1, 2, 3, 4 and 5.

Local Education Authority (LEA)

The local government body responsible for providing education for all learners of compulsory school age. The LEA is also responsible for managing the education budget for 16–19 learners in its area.

Mandatory units

These are units that all learners must complete to gain a qualification; in this case a BTEC Level 3 National. Some BTEC qualifications have an over-arching title, eg Construction, but within Construction you can choose different pathways. Your chosen pathway may have additional mandatory units specific to that pathway.

Mentor

A more experienced person who will guide you, and counsel you if you have a problem or difficulty.

Mode of delivery

The way in which a qualification is offered to learners for example, part-time, full-time, as a short course or by distance learning.

National Occupational Standard (NOS)

Statements of the skills, knowledge and understanding you need to develop in order to be competent at a particular job.

National Vocational Qualification (NVQ)

Qualifications that concentrate on the practical skills and knowledge required to do a job competently. They are usually assessed in the workplace and range from Level 1 (the lowest) to Level 5 (the highest).

Nested qualifications

Qualifications that have 'common' units, so that learners can easily progress from one to another by adding on more units.

Ofqual

The public body responsible for regulating qualifications, exams and tests in England.

Optional units

Units on your course from which you may be able to make a choice. They help you specialise your skills, knowledge and understanding and may help progression into work or further education.

Pathway

All BTEC Level 3 National qualifications comprise a small number of mandatory units and a larger number of optional units. These units are grouped into different combinations to provide alternative pathways to achieving the qualification. These pathways are usually linked to different career preferences.

Peer review

This involves feedback on your performance by your peers (members of your team, or class group.) You will also be given an opportunity to review their performance.

Plagiarism

The practice of copying someone else's work, or work from any other sources (eg the internet), and passing it off as your own. This practice is strictly forbidden on all courses.

Personal, learning and thinking skills (PLTS)

The skills, personal qualities and behaviour that improve your ability to work independently. Developing these skills makes you more effective and confident at work. Opportunities for developing these skills are a feature of all BTEC Level 3 National courses. These skills aren't compulsory to achieve on the course, but are of great use to you.

Portfolio

A collection of work compiled by a learner, usually as evidence of learning, to present to an assessor.

Procrastinator

Someone who is forever putting off or delaying work, either because they are lazy or because they have poor organisational skills.

Professional body

An organisation that exists to promote or support a particular profession; for example, the Royal Institute of British Architects (RIBA).

Professional development and training

This involves undertaking activities relevant to your job to increase and/or update your knowledge and skills.

Project

A project is a comprehensive piece of work, which normally involves original research and investigation by an individual or by a team. The findings and results may be presented in writing and summarised as a presentation.

Qualifications and Credit Framework (QCF)

The QCF is a framework for recognising skills and qualifications. It does this by awarding credit for qualifications and units so that they are easier to measure and compare. All BTEC Level 3 National qualifications are part of the QCF.

Qualifications and Curriculum Development Agency (QCDA)

The QCDA is responsible for maintaining and developing the national curriculum, delivering assessments, tests and examinations and reforming qualifications.

Quality assurance

In education, this is the process of continually checking that a course of study is meeting the specific requirements set down by the awarding body.

Sector Skills Councils (SSCs)

The 25 employer-led, independent organisations responsible for improving workforce skills in the UK by identifying skill gaps and improving learning in the workplace. Each council covers a different type of industry.

Semester

Many universities and colleges divide their academic year into two halves or semesters, one from September to January and one from February to July.

Seminar

A learning event involving a group of learners and a tutor, which may be learner-led, and follow research into a topic that has been introduced at an earlier stage.

Study buddy

A person in your group or class who takes notes for you and keeps you informed of important developments if you are absent. You do the same for them in return.

Time-constrained assignment

An assessment you must complete within a fixed time limit.

Tutorial

An individual or small group meeting with your tutor at which you can discuss your current work and other more general course issues. At an individual tutorial, your progress on the course will be discussed and you can raise any concerns or personal worries you may have.

The University and Colleges Admissions Service (UCAS)

UCAS (pronounced 'you-cass') is the central organisation that processes all applications for higher education (HE) courses.

UCAS points

The number of points allocated by UCAS for the qualifications you have obtained. Higher education institutions specify how many points you need to be accepted on the courses they offer. See page 96 to find out how to access a website where you can find out more.

Unit abstract

The summary at the start of each BTEC unit that tells you what the unit is about.

Unit content

Details about the topics covered by the unit and the knowledge and skills you need to complete it.

Unit points

The number of points you gain when you complete a unit. These will depend on the grade you achieve (pass, merit or distinction).

Vocational qualification

Designed to develop knowledge and understanding relevant to a chosen area of work.

Work experience

Time you spend on an employer's premises when you learn about the enterprise, carry out work-based tasks and develop skills and knowledge.

Please note that all information given within these useful terms was correct at the time of going to print.